The Majestic Columbia River Gorge

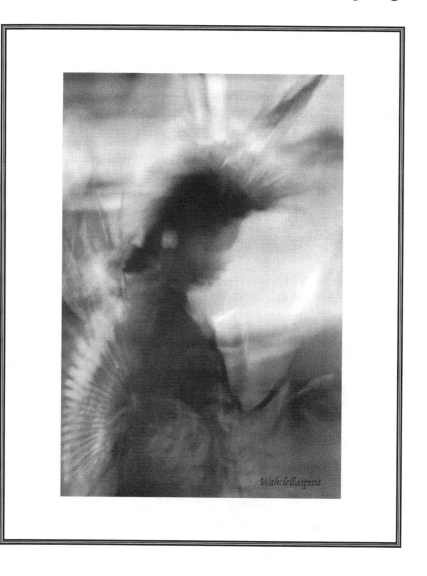

Wahclellaspini

A Journey Treasured Throughout Time
A Cooley Cultus Potlatch Hyas Ahnkuttie

To order additional copies of this book, contact:
Xlibris Corporation
1-888-795-4274
www.Xlibris.com
Orders@Xlibris.com
120933

The Majestic

Columbia

River Gorge

By Wahclellaspirit

The Majestic Columbia River Gorge A Journey Treasured Throughout Time

A Cooley Cultus Potlatch Kopa Hyas Ahnkuttie

A Fictional Writing and Photographic Guide Through the Valley of the Eagle, and Into the Lands of Wah Within the Columbia River Gorge in Oregon and Washington.

Author and Photographer
Wahclellaspirit

I dedicate this book to Kevin Fall, my close friend and fellow hiker with whom I shared many days on the trails of the Oregon and Washington Cascades in exploration of the Pacific Northwest's geological events, past and present. Kevin now resides on Mt. Shasta, California, from where he smiles down on those of us who have yet to reach his plateau.

Kevin Fall
1954-2010

Table of Contents

Image Locations per Chapters

The Majestic Columbia River Gorge

This book, The Majestic Columbia River Gorge, was written in an attempt to share with you the mystique, the serenity and the breathtaking beauty of the numerous Gorge waterfalls and the surrounding lands that whisper a fascinating history of the Columbia River Gorge Scenic Area.

While on frequent hikes and photographic adventures throughout the Columbia River Gorge, my imagination, facts—and lore—that I've gleaned from history sources, have been an enormous enjoyment to me. Enough so that I want to share it with you. Even though the present majesty and beauty of the Gorge lands is obvious now, sometimes even magical, I imagine them at a different time in the long ago, how they may have appeared during the days when the Great Chinook Nation thrived here.

I had completed a good part of my writing when, while researching on the internet, I discovered the historic and beautiful bit of prose written by Chief Seattle to the Great White Chief in Washington after an offer had been presented to the Suquamish Tribe in 1854. The plan was to obtain two million acres for the sum of $150,000.00 and a land reservation for the Tribe. Chief Seattle expressed a premonition that the lands that once offered food and sustenance to all who lived upon them, would become desecrated and depleted by mankind's greed for money and power. He expressed his belief that this would destroy and interfere with the Spirits that have inhabited the earth from the beginning of time.

One day, our generation will also be a part of this region's history as are the Native Americans that had once inhabited and those that still reside along the banks of the Columbia. Through the efforts of many, hopefully these lands will remain detached from encroachment.

Hopefully these majestic lands, through wisdom and integrity, will be preserved. Hopefully all life that has and is safely existing now, will continue to live in peace and in harmony with one another, and the Land's of Wah's earth rhythm will survive and escape so-called "progress".

Imagine the solitary call of the coyote in search of her mate as we travel along the many intertwining trails of the Gorge lands. Imagine you are entering before the Hallowed Walls of Wahclella to worship with the Spirits of past legends as they remind us of the necessity of saving our sanctified earth, treating it with respect and taking only what we absolutely need. To give thanks to the earth for giving us what we need.

Imagine yourself reaching for the stars as you crest the top of The Great Larch Mountain and gaze about the Kingdom of Wah.

I will lead you, through these stories, following the paths that lead through the Valley of the Eagle and into the Lands of Wah.

I hope that you will also find yourself standing in awe of what nature has presented us, and that you will keep the Valley of the Eagle and the Lands of Wah, these ancient and formidable lands clean and sacred, as they have been throughout the many years past.

Each and every cascade embraces a story that reveals its history. It is up to us, as individuals, to be perceptive and allow our senses to become one with nature and truly find their significance in our lives!

Mitlite Okoke Kloshe Tahmahnawis Kopa Mika . . . .

May The Good Spirits Be With You . . . .

Waterfalls of The Valley of the Eagle

All waterfalls begin at trailhead at end of parking area at Eagle Creek Trail and distances are one way only.

(1.) Metlako Falls—108 feet high—1.50 miles and approximately 50 minutes from trailhead.

(2.) Punch Bowl Falls—50 feet high—1.90 miles and approximately 1 hour tolower viewpoint—2.10 miles and 1 1/4 hours to higher viewpoint.

(3.) Loowit Falls—125 high—3.20 miles and approximately 2 hours to viewpoint.

(4.) Skoonichuk Falls—30 high—4.0 miles and 3 hours to top of falls.

(5.) Tunnel Falls—120 high—6.20 miles and 5 1/4 hours.

(6.) Eagle Creek Falls—110 high—6.75 miles and 5 1/2 hours.

Waterfalls of the Land's of Wah

(1.) Munra Falls—60 feet high—1/4 mile and 10 minutes from Wahclella Falls or Tanner Creek parking area.

(2.) Wahclella Falls—125 feet high—1 mile and 45 minutes from trailhead.

(3.) Elowah Falls—289 feet high—.80 mile and 20 minutes from trailhead at McCord Creek or Elowah parking lot.

(4.) Upper McCord Creek Falls—100 feet high—1.10 miles and 35 minutes from trailhead.

(5.) Horsetail Falls—176 feet high—Abutting Columbia River Gorge National Scenic Highway.

(6.) Ponytail Falls—125 feet high—.30 mile and 20 minutes from parking at Horsetail Parking.

(7.) Upper Oneonta Falls—55 feet high—1.20 miles and 47 minutes from Horsetail Falls Parking.

(8.) Triple Falls—135 feet high—2.20 miles and 1 1/2 hours from Horsetail Falls parking.

(9.) Oneonta Falls—100 feet high—1/4 mile through Oneonta Gorge abutting Columbia River Gorge National ScenicHighway.

Waterfalls of the Land's of Wah

Waterfalls numbered 10-14 are on Multnomah Falls to Wahkeena Falls Loop, and parking is along the Columbia River Gorge National Scenic Highway or at the Multnomah Falls Parking area between lanes on Interstate 84, exit 31.

(10.) Little Multnomah Falls—15 feet high—1.10 miles and 50 minutes from parking lot at Multnomah Falls.

(11.) Multnomah Falls—620 feet high—1.10 miles and 50 minutes to top of falls.

(12.) Dutchman Falls—50 feet high—1.20 miles and 57 minutes.

(13.) Weisendanger Falls—90 feet high—1.40 miles and 1 hour.

(14.) Hidden Falls—80 feet high—1.60 miles and 1 hour 25 minutes.

All parking for waterfalls numbered 15-21 is along Columbia River Gorge National Scenic Highway.

(15.) *Fairy Falls—30 feet high—1.10 miles and 1 hour 10 minutes from Wahkeena Falls Parking.*

(16.) *Wahkeena Falls—242 feet high—Abutting Columbia River Gorge National ScenicHighway.*

(17.) *Coopey Falls—175 feet high—.50 mile and 17 minutes from Angels Rest Trailhead.*

(18.) *Bridal Veil Falls—160 feet high—3/4 mile and 15 minutes from parking at Bridal Veil Park.*

(19.) *Sheppards Dell Falls—125 feet high—Abutting Highway.*

(20.) *Latourell Falls—249 feet high—Abutting Highway.*

(21.) *Upper Latourell Falls—100 feet high—1 mile and 30 minutes to base of falls.*

Preface
Our Inevitable Escape

This is the story of my peoples' perilous trek to these lands. My grandfather stated that many suns had passed since our people stood proud before the slavish Chief of our homeland declaring their disgust and outrage. My people told of constantly being robbed of their blankets and goods that they used for bartering with other tribes. My grandfather told of the harshness of the plains, and of the Great Spirits that manage life and death, of the promise to us that if we honored and respected the lands and waters, that all of our brothers, all of our people would continue to be welcome.

As our people innocently believed, as they lived in reverence, the savage Chief that reigned the vastness of these plains, and his band of followers, maliciously continued to pillage our people's villages and prevent their efforts to provide for themselves and live in peace. The intruders would arrive suddenly, without warning, and our people would be left with nothing. I was told that with the passing of many moons, the leaders of our many villages began to gather and form alliances with one another. Even so, our villages were continually ravaged until they were forced to flee.

Our families then crossed the great waters and set their course across the frozen lands that stood unsettled and unwelcoming. Our people continued undaunted. After many years, they discovered a great river in new lands that were foreign to them. These lands are now known as the Cascades and the mighty river is named the Columbia.

Our people are now secure across the remote lands of these Cascades and the Great Salt Chuck. It is along the Creek of the Eagle, which joins with the Columbia, that this story begins.

Pahto

Long ago, before the arrival of the white man, it was the desire of the Great Spirit that we still believe in today that created the majestic snow cloaked peaks of the Cascades, and the incarnation of the Spirit People.

The Spirit took the form of the sun, and as it rose day after day alone from the faraway lands of the east and set upon the trails of the west, Hyas Otelagh, Sun, found himself desiring companionship. Several of the Cascades would rise to meet him as he passed overhead, and these members of the Cascade family would soon become his brides.

However, when Sun beheld the massive mountain below him as he toured overhead, he gave it life and caused it to rise towards the sanctity of the heavens.

This glorious member of the Cascade family Sun would name as his son, Pahto, that is defined as meaning Standing High.

Sun chose for Pahto to meet him upon the good spirits of first light and to stay with him until the bad spirits that thrive during night arose from the edge of darkness.

As each season passed Sun greeted Pahto each and every day, bathing him in the bright morning light, and at the end of the day, it was Pahto to whom the Great Spirit bid, "peace to you my son, and await for my arrival from the land's of the east upon first light."

All the blessings of strength, magnificence, and power did Sun bestow on his son Pahto.

So the Great Spirit joyfully created offspring. The Spirit went as far as to commit the care and safety of his own wives to the powerful Pahto.

For many days there was peace across the lands that Pahto stood proud upon, then one day, the first wife of Sun, Plastakh, became jeolous of Pahto's powers and of his favor before Sun.

Plastakh was heard to ask her sisters, "Who is Pahto that we are to be found subject to his will?"

The mountain brides were then quickly found to be uncertain of their sister as they feared the mighty powers of Pahto, as they too desired to please the Great Sun.

Yet Pastakh denied to honor Sun and denounced the grounds that Pahto ruled!

Let us not bring Pahto berries or game to fill his table. We must gather all the elk and deer, the bear and the salmon, and keep these spirits for ourselves to bring us honor amongst all those that tread upon our trails.

Upon the rise of first light Pahto journeyed to Sun's brides for his daily morning meal, and it was then that Plastakh was heard to scream, "Pahto, journey through the lands that we, the brides of Sun protect, and hunt your own meals as they are now hidden from your sight. We, my sisters and I, are the brides of Sun, not yours! So seek your meals from another's table!

Pahto became hungrier as Plastakh continued to shout of her disgust, and as Pahto attempted to reason with the brides of Sun he stated unto Plastakh,

All of you, the brides of Sun were placed under my protection by my Father's will. You all know your obligation and duties to recieve my protection from the Evil Spirits that resist the trails that we journey. Each one of you must not resist the word of Sun! I shall forgive you all if you now place my meal before me and allow me to eat in silence.

As Pahto spoke to Sun's brides Plastakh became infuriated and began to shriek insults towards Pahto, and as Pahto stood in silence Plastakh stepped in front of him and slapped him hard across the crown of the head.

The mighty Pahto quickly filled with anger at Plastakh's dismissal and quickly began to shake and rumble, and then erupted fiery rock and emitted smoke upon his displeasure!

Upon Pahto's show of temper the ground began to shake violently, and the great forests of Cedar and Firs were quickly set ablaze.

Sun's brides were quickly found fearful as they realized that they had wrongly overlooked Pahto's immense powers that were given him by Sun, as Pahto began to boil in anger and spread across the lands his vengeance.

There were three brides of Sun that fled across the Great River and sought safety with the smoking warrior God, Wy-East. These three brides of Sun could be heard to scream and plead before the Great Wy-East,

We have offended Sun, and now Pahto has taken from us the peace we once found upon the grounds of your family, and we have journeyed across the blackened ruins of Pahto's lands, and have no land where we can each find peace.

Wy-East looked down upon Klah Klahnee with compassion, and as he stood proud upon the highest ridge he stated, "You and your sisters may journey through my lands in safety and find peace wherever you choose to rest! Find yourself the best rivers and valleys and forests that rise beneath me, and they will be yours to discover and prosper. But you must be assured to respect my word, for I am the Great Warrior of these lands!"

As the three brides settled upon Wy-East's lands, Pahto had severely beaten Plastakh and left her in ruin.

As Sun rose from upon the plain of the lands and arose into the heavens he peered down unto the lands that Pahto ruled and witnessed to the devestation of his kingdom that Pahto had chosen to allow.

Vanished from the lands beneath Sun were the game, the fish, and all the lush valleys where the Animal People once lived in peace. Upon these same grounds that were once filled with life were now seen by Sun infused with huge streams of hissing rock and the blackened remains of all life that could not escape Pahto's fury.

To look upon the grounds that he himself gave to Pahto destroyed did notanger Sun to the degree of punishing him before all the peoples of the lands. But when he saw that Pahto had demolished Plastakh, his favored bride, and had left her in ruins, angered him immensely.

Sun quickly peered across all the lands beneath him and saw that three of his brides had fled and found sanctuary alongside the land's of Wy-East. Sun then approached the lands that Wy-East ruled and stated unto him,

"You have been ever faithful and just before these lands. It is good that you have given haven to Klah Klahnee and the others, so I ask of you the Great Warrior Wy-East to go and punish Pahto upon his own grounds, and what is now his shall soon be yours forever."

Upon the Great Sun's plead Wy-East quickly armed himself and delivered battle to Pahto.

For many days the battle between Pahto and Wy-East was fiercely fought, and at one point Pahto smote Wy-East on the back that kindled Wy-East's anger to rise and fume. Great showers of molten rock and fire were spent upon the grounds of Pahto, and Pahto lie injured and remorseful for his temper toward Plastakh.

The battle between the two continued for many days, and one day Wy-East struck Pahto and shattered his proud crown, and was then awarded victor of the intense battle between the two giants.

Throughout the lengthy battle between them, Sun and the mountain people had watched the fiery combat as it spread across the skies, and they were much pleased in Wy-East's victory!

Yet Wy-East was gracious in his victory and took compassion upon the lost spirit of his foe, and he began to speak to Pahto,

"All you have and had has been awarded to me by Sun. I could leave you cold and desolate without the companionship of any animal people."

At this, Pahto's crown began to weep and rain down across the slopes and he pleaded before Wy-East and to the Great Sun as the heavens above also rained down upon them for many days, and he found regret given his behavior before Wy-East!

Sun then went off to the lands of Wy-East and asked him of what he thought he should do with Pahto, upon their meeting, Wy-East was heard to have stated,

"I will restore half of Pahto's streams and rivers and lakes. I will also give him a third of all the game and berries that once found rise upon his lands. But Pahto will have no one for companionship, except for the remains of Plastakh whom he has so sadly abused. And this shall be found just from this day to the last that the Great Sun crosses over the remaining family of the Cascades."

And Sun was then greatly pleased with Wy-East's favor!

Upon Wy-East's kind heart, Sun also found forgiveness and approached Pahto with words spelled with wisdom;

"The mighty Wy-East has had mercy on your spirit! Some of what was yours will be returned, you will be saddened by my decision in that I have chose to allow the mountain people to find repose upon Wy-East's lands and far from your own."

As Sun spoke to Pahto, Pahto lie moaning in his defeat before all the mountain people, he eventually calmed and asked the Great Sun,

"But my head my Great Father, what of my head?"

Sun considered Pahto's question as he passed overhead seven times, and then upon the eighth pass over the sullen Pahto he exclaimed to his son;

"I shall give you a new crown, as you have asked. But as a condition of my favor, you shall forever care for the Plastakh, and you shall never travel upon the trails that lead to the mountain people's lands again!"

And so it was from that day forward!

Pahto's new crown was named White Eagle, and Sun caused flows of molten rock to anchor the once Great Pahto again upon the earth.

To this day, Pahto presents a flattened crown upon his head while Wy-East rises proudly above his own lands that lead to the shores of the Great River.

The three brides were honored to the lands to the south of Wy-East, and they dwell in safety between other mountain peoples.

This is all that remains of Plastakh, the once favored bride of Sun. Today she rests in peace and in harmony within her sanctuary in silence, and far from the shadows of Pahto's reign.

The Lost Spirits of Pahto's Broken Stones

Our people prospered under Pahto's rule for many moons. We found comfort and safety beside the Great Spirit. Our people's souls were held high before him. We honored and respected our lands and ask for his guidance, ask him to protect us from the evil spirits that lie in wait for our souls when we feel weak or wander from our beliefs. We trusted in Pahto's strength and guidance as we journeyed across the lands of Sun, Our Great Earth Spirit.

Then upon one passing of Sun, the land beneath the mighty Pahto began to tremble. It is here that the story of the Spirits of Broken Stones began. It started with an inner challenge to the detachment and weakness of Pahto's soul. These weakened moments allowed the evil spirits to be in control. This was the beginning to the fall of the great wall from his frozen face that once held strong to his whitened scalp.

Because of his power, from the time of his birth upon the lands of the Cascades, Pahto was consistently challenged. The great Sun had breathed life beneath the soils that gave rise to the Great Pahto. As the Sun crossed the heavens, Pahto grew and became even more powerful. His spirit was constantly challenged and influenced by the evil spirits. But his spirit remained strong and this allowed him to grow tall and mighty amidst the thinning air of the heavens.

The time came when The Great Pahto let his guard down. He became impressed with his power. It was an opening for these challenging spirits to tempt Pahto, in his most weakest of times. These spirits tore at his soul and wrought devastation upon his kingdom.

Pahto suddenly lost his temper. He trembled violently through the heat of his rage at the spirits as they continued.

Pahto tried to remain untroubled before his clan but he had become weak. The spirits were persistent. They wanted to destroy Pahto and because he did not use his inner spirit and strengths, they were slowly succeeding. Pahto exploded in anger many times and tried to cast the evil spirits from beneath him and towards the depths of the Great River. However, they returned time and time again only to exercise their powers against Pahto once again. These spirits had promised Pahto that they would hold strong against the lands of his kingdom and that they would devastate all that he held sacred.

Pahto eventually chased the evil spirits from beneath him and he then grew silent for many seasons. Again he chose to stand tall and keep peace amongst his tribe. Sun crossed overhead many times as he returned to his village in the east, and as he looked down at his creation, he smiled as Pahto stood silent and reached higher to the heavens. Sun had challenged Pahto to hold his temper before the evil spirits without his knowing. As Pahto now stood in peace, Sun hoped that one day he would grow strong and wise in the ways of the Great Chiefs that ruled above all the Cascades. Pahto would then be one in spirit, and he would deliver kindness before all those that found their way before him, and in peace, all life would survive bountifully within the mighty kingdom that rested below him.

The evil spirits chose to lie in wait. They were allured by the kingdom's bounty that brought forth great numbers of our people. The animal spirits, as well, gathered in great numbers within the open meadows. The forests, the birds, the elk and deer, and all living animals that are gifts from the Great Sun were again gathered in great numbers.

And, as Sun had promised, the lands were again whole.

Many suns passed over Pahto's lands. The evil spirit's numbers became stronger within him. Their heated breath began to rise slowly above Pahto's crown. From deep within the soul of Pahto could be heard the chants of the bad spirits rising from Pahto's dome. They challenged Pahto in his resolve to uphold the wishes of the Great Earth Spirit.

Pahto had become complacent and was not listening to his inner spirit. He had no warning of the evil spirit's craving for his soul. He had been standing in silence and had caused peace to enter within him for many seasons. The silence of the evil ones had lain dormant beneath him. They chose their battle well.

And then the battle began again . . .

The ground began to shudder and tremble with great fury. The animals and people that had chosen these lands for their villages were shaken by the increasing number of angered rumbles that were cast from above them. Great smoke was lifted high to the heavens. Many animal spirits fled the kingdom in fright of the evil one's putrid breaths. Soon there were few living creatures that desired to live beneath Pahto's frequent expulsions.

Our people fled to the valleys below the beautiful Tehoma, and towards the kingdom of the Raven. It has been told that Sun led many of our people to find sanctity within Wy-East's kingdom. Our people were spread across all the lands of the Cascades, and many of our brothers and sisters were not found. We were a people without a village, and we felt disgraced and discouraged before Sun. Pahto had swiftly chosen our dismissal upon these lands that had been promised to us. We were defeated, and as we chose the trails that led away from our villages we held our heads low as we were now outcasts living within another village, and within the kingdom of other's lands.

There could be heard across all the kingdoms of the Cascades that Pahto had again chosen to wail before them, and that he had failed the lessons that Sun had chosen for him.

The Great Tehoma feared Pahto. He knew that if Pahto did not refuse temptation and win the battle, that the bad spirits would then feed upon that weakness and gain strength in their numbers. He considered that his kingdom might also be attacked by the powers of the evil spirits. In numbers that had never been seen before.

Lawala Clough stood dismayed by Pahto's fume. She had chosen him to be hers. She felt shame for her wanting and she lay her head low in dishonor and shame. As Pahto chased the evil spirits from beneath him, he was causing great fires and floods that were laying ruin to the lands that surrounded him. Through his weaknessess—anger and jealousy, he was destroying his own kingdom!

Wy-East knew that if Pahto's soul continued to be swollen with anger and jealousy of Wy-East's silence, that he might again thrust the heated spears that were lying within his soul. As it became apparent that Pahto chose to lay ruin to his lands, Wy-East felt he might, himself, need to defend against this raid, rise up the valley floors, and challenge the breaths of Pahto. Wy-East felt that he would need to flood all the lands of Pahto's kingdom and leave Pahto's spirit drowned and left deep beneath the seething waters.

High upon Pahto's crown could be heard the screams from the rock spirits as they were forced to fall upon the lands below.

The High Spirits of the Cascades then knew that Pahto was challenging the evil spirits, and that soon they would need to join forces to protect all of their lands from the heated breaths of the evil spirits.

37

All the Great Spirits that grew tall alongside Pahto's kingdom waited unhurried and swore before him that he must challenge his soul, gain strength to battle the evil spirits within himself, and not release his anger across their lands.

As Sun passed overhead again and again, he looked beneath him, and Sun spoke to Pahto with the same wisdom. Pahto continued to vent and rage, and was soon engulfed by the inferno cast from within his distempered soul.

As Wy-East stood and awaited Pahto's angry charges on his kingdom, he saw that the soul of Pahto had begun to crumble and fail. It toppled from above the valley's floor, a dark cloud that held the broken spirits of Pahto's stone arose from beside his devastated spirit, and they did not cling to his face again.

The lost spirits now soared higher than Pahto's unseen peak, and all the Great Spirits of the Cascades knelt before their lands and cried before their peoples. Before all the animal spirits they wept.

The battle within Pahto for his soul had begun. The days grew darker as Sun was not seen above the kingdoms of the Cascades. All the Great Spirits of the Cascades could not see the battle that then raged across Pahto's kingdom. Only the cries of the broken stones would be heard crashing down upon the valley's floor.

The echo of the spirit's cries were then lost to our peoples and to the lands that we once coveted. The cries fell upon the ears of Wy-East, Lawala Clough, and the Great Tehoma, and sadness pierced their souls.

The Great Spirits knew then that the warmth that Sun had once fastened upon his side would not fall across the lands for many moons, and for that time, the great forests and plains would not surrender nourishment to people and animal spirits to keep them strong for their journeys and survival.

The High Spirits of the Cascades knew that the cold winds of Illahee, cold winter, would soon fall upon them, and many of their peoples would then be lost. They knew that Salmon would not enter the fast waters of the Great River from beneath the kingdom of the setting sun, and their spirits would also be cast aside and be lost to our people. They also knew that the mowitch and moolock would flee the lands, and they too would submit to the cold breaths of winter as their spirits would lie frozen upon the hardened and barren grounds.

The kingdoms that they knew were becoming void of life and of good spirit. They knew also that they would soon become one with the bad spirits if Pahto did not hold within his tempered brow the heated breaths that had many times scorched the lands, the same lands that had since allowed our souls to prosper through the teachings and wisdom of the High Spirit.

Pahto must allow our people to stand below Sun once again as it is he that gives us life. They knew that if, in Pahto's storm, he did not hear their cries, they too would discover their spirits beyond the entrance to the Great Sea, and lost.

And our peoples would then be no longer!

Sun would again be challenged to begin anew with peoples that would claim the lands as their own. It was feared that they would be filled with the evil spirits, and with those troubled souls, they would become greedy and disregard the animal spirits and the souls of the sticks as they grew strong above them, and the spirits that Sun would choose to live within Pahto's kingdom would not honor the sacred lands.

These lands could not survive!

Sun appeared upon the horizon as he toured across all the lands of our brother's nations, and there was heard a great clap of thunder that began without first casting the heated spears from the heaven's emblazoned trails.

Wy-east and the Hyas Tehoma stood angered at what they saw of Pahto's disregard for the sanctity of the kingdoms of the High Spirits of the Cascades.

Wy-East remembered of the spears that had once been cast upon his lands because of Pahto's disgust at losing the battle for Lawala Clough. Wy-East stood steadfastly upon his mount and waited to spear Pahto's soul. Only then would the Great Sun allow the kingdoms of the Cascades to once again lie silent and prosper.

Much was learned from Pahto's battle about inner strength and power. The Evil Spirits were cast out. From the valley floors could be heard the cries of the Evil Spirits that had once clung to the kingdom that Pahto had grown. As they coursed across the lands, their cries were increasingly repeated before their souls had turned to dust and fell silent upon their execution.

And their spirits were never again heard nor seen within the kingdom.

The Lost Spirits of Pahto's Broken Stones had turned to dust, but it is now known that from that dust arose a great forest, and that the animal spirits beneath the stick's covering arms are again thriving. The grasses and hedges are thick, and every day as they await the return of Sun to rise high into the heavens, Sun has seen that the spirits Pahto had once held tightly upon his face now gave life upon the lands.

Pahto's temper wavered and he lost respect before Sun and all the High Spirits of the Cascades. Eventually Pahto gained the wisdom *of the Cascades. He once again stood proud and silent, peering across his kingdom. He learned then that the battle within his soul could be cast far from his heights, and the Spirits held within him destroyed without the advent of fire or flood spread across his kingdom. He had been honored with protecting his lands and all that lived upon them. He once failed but then he learned of strength, wishing not to disrupt the spirits of the great lands.*

The Great Sun gave a lesson to Pahto. He listened to his Inner Spirit and learned.

Great Earth Spirit and his peoples would now prosper and survive for all time from that day forward.

The Chief and the Angry White Mountain

It was in a time of our forefathers long ago that Skookum Tumtum, Brave Heart, was chief of our peoples amongst the lands called the Wisscopam. Brave Heart was a wise and knowledgeable leader, many stories that have been told before our campfires have stated that he was a man that was held to mystic visions and knew of the Spirit of the Great White Peak that rises to the south and west.

Sollecks Tkope Lamotai, Angry White Mountain, is the guardian mountain for Brave Heart and our lands, and the Hyas Tumtum, Great Spirit, had given Sollecks Tkope Lamotai dominion over the land that crosses through the heart of the Cascades and the valley that holds to the Great River.

The peak was also the birthplace that held many of the bad spirits within its calloused and evil soul, skookum tumtum. Upon Coyote's journeys across the distant lands and far from the slopes of the Great White Mountain one of these skookum spirits would break free of the angry mountain's bonds, and as it was not able to take on human form would cause the Great White Mountain to shake and rumble, and to fill the sky above with burning and steaming rock.

The White Mountain would echo its mastery unto our people's fears for many suns and moons that crossed the trails of our skies, and after the bad spirit had chosen to claim the great snows upon its peak, he left only black and burnt rock in his footsteps as the bad spirit once again fell silent upon Coyote's lingered turn.

Bound again within the bowels of the fuming demon spirit's village, the Mesachie Tumtum would lie silent and await the day that

Coyote chose to journey across the snowfields that grace the White Mountain to our south to speak to our brothers that lie west where the spirit of the ehkolie, whale, jumps from the deep waters.

Brave Heart and his people were blessed by the Great Spirit. They grew strong and healthy and gave thanks for the spirit of the moolock, elk, and salmon that favored their tables. They gave thanks for the souls of the eena, beaver, that warmed their souls through the winter's freeze, and they gave thanks for the chakchak, eagle, as their spirits graced the sky above them and fed from the waters that they themselves found food.

As the snows of the winter flowed into the falling waters of the White Mountain many young braves gathered high upon the open slopes in search of their own Thunder Dreams. They would chant the stories of our people's survival upon the demon spirits of the mountain, and the mountain would then answer with rumblings from beneath its soils. The braves would find themselves fasting as the sun crossed overhead for many days, and it is here that Brave Heart first envisioned a dream as was passed to him from our Great Forefathers who also once stood upon this very peak and chanted unto the spirit world.

Brave Heart stood upon the mountain one day as the colors of the trees and bushes began to turn bright with yellows and reds, and it was then that he saw the pointed arrowhead that held the bad spirits inside the depths of the peak fall beneath to the mountain's floor.

Suddenly there was a great shaking and blackened rings of smoke arose from the angry spirit's belly. As Brave Heart stood silent and in terror to the Mesachie Spirit's claim to the mountain, large rivers of fire rock freely flowed upon his lands and quieted the call of the elk and bear, and scorched the valleys of all life as great smokes arose to cover the sky above.

As tears fell silent from Brave Heart's face the voice of Coyote began to fill the air. Though Brave Heart felt dismissed by the good spirit as his lands were not spared, he listened intently to the wise words of his *Hyas Tumtum, High Spirit*.

"From this day forward, the heights that you now stand, and the lands beyond your sights shall not be tread. The men and women of your village shall not visit upon these soils again!

It is by my wisdom that you must obey these words that I do now speak!

If I find your people honorable and distant from this mountain, all shall be well within you,

Be strong and walk amongst your peoples and guide them from the *klale tumtum, black heart,* of this mountain, and we will one day meet again, and the lands beyond these traces shall offer your peoples their treasures as you had once collected.

I, Coyote, has now spoken!"

Brave Heart was so honored that Coyote had spoken to him that he fled the mountaintop and gathered the families of his village from each of the distant valleys and ridges.

Brave Heart sat before the fire of his people's camp and told of the vision he had encountered as he had stood above the demon spirit's village upon the Great White Mountain. Upon finishing the vision's truths as he had seen and was then told by Coyote his people gathered beside him and they fled from the mountain and entered the land that held the hidden lake of the Sacred Elk Spirit.

Upon entering the land of the hidden lake of the Sacred Elk Spirit Brave Heart soon noticed that his son Thunder Heart was not present, Brave Heart had no fear for his son as he too was a great warrior and was promised to his hunt amongst the land of the Klickitats.

Brave Heart sent a messenger to find Thunder Heart to tell him of the vision and for him to cross the Great River and join his father as they were soon to find shelter far from the angry mountain.

As Thunder Heart arrived before the valley where his people's lived, his wife, Moolock Klootchman, Elk Woman, ran out to meet him and began to speak of their troubles.

"The Great Spirit Coyote has revealed that the Bad Spirits are angry with our people. Unless the spirits of the White Mountain can be defeated, our peoples shall not survive amongst these lands!"

Thunder Heart quickly ran up the valley only to see many families fleeing over a distant ridge to the west, and the guardian mountain steaming and looming in disgust in the distance.

Thunder Heart asked Elk Woman what his father spoke of the vision?

Elk Woman then told Thunder Heart that his father commanded him to fight and slay the mountain's demonic spirits. She also told him to go quickly upon the mountain's highest peak and that his father would join him and they would fight the spirits together.

Upon given this tale from Elk Woman, Thunder Heart set out for the mountain unaware of her selfish ploy.

The legend cast by our tribe tells that Elk Woman wished to be known as a sacred woman of our clan, and the wife of a sacred warrior hero.

As quickly as Thunder Heart said farewell to Elk Woman and began to climb upon the mountain, Elk Woman fled across the divide and found shelter along the banks of the sacred lake.

Through the darkness that the evil spirits rise from the soils of the earth, Thunder Heart climbed towards the summit of the Great White Mountain. As the sun arose upon the crest of the highest ridge he neared the crater that held the bad spirits. It was there that he quietly stood before it and began to chant a spell that told the spirits of his intent to slay their souls and to make his lands safe from their ruse.

As the sun rose to its highest peak Thunder Heart thought back to the story Elk Woman told him and of his father, Brave Heart, joining him to find battle between the evil ones. He stood there peering deep into the blackened soul of the beasts as they spewed hot gasses and small rocks from beneath their shelter, and it was then that Thunder Heart began to understand that he must now battle the Mesachie Tumtums alone if they were to survive.

Quickly he stood before the venting of the spirit's anger and placed an arrow from his quiver upon the vine of his bow and fired intently into the heart of the beast. As he fired again and again the spirits rumbled with roars of anger that could be heard across the Great River, and sadly they fell upon those ears that fled far into the distant valleys.

As Thunder Heart continued to unfurl arrows into the demon's soul one arrow severed the bonds of all the evil spirits from the mountain, and not even Coyote could instill fear into their evil souls and hold them beneath the molten rock and soils that now fumed with their stink.

Without warning the earth and mountains and valleys from all around began to tremble, and as Thunder Heart fell back, the rock that once stood tall beside him opened and spewed black smoke as the mountain began to breach from within the blackened hole that freed the souls of the bad spirits.

Fire rocks and steam were again cast far into the heavens and upon the trails that lead to our Forefather's village.

Loud noises from within the belly of the spirit then marked the beginning of the battle for the lands beneath the Great White Mountain, and there stood Thunder Heart once again firing his arrows into the heart of the angered beasts within.

As Thunder Heart fought on through the night the battle slowed, and the fire's that gave strength to the mighty beast of the Bad Spirit cooled, and he chose to sit and rest before the final battle began.

"Thunder Heart!

Your people were told by your father's vision and by my wise words you were not to tread upon these soils again! Your peoples were lectured not to linger upon the soils of this mountain's roar, but to leave these lands and claim upon the valleys distant to these your peoples had once claimed.

Be wise Thunder Heart, and flee these lands! For I Coyote can not stop the spirit's heated breaths from reaching the soils beneath its fiery stream."

Thunder Heart was a brave warrior, and he continued to fight the spirits for many suns and moons. Far distant from the battle, Thunder Heart's people stood and watched in horror and dread as the mountain roared, and Elk Woman stood smiling and silently awaiting to become legend amongst their tribe.

As each day passed the battle became more fierce, and on the evening of the sixth pass of Sun, Thunder Heart seemed to have won the battle as the mountain grew silent once again.

Thunder Heart again chose to sit and rest upon the Great White Mountain that was now stained with black rock and the souls of the bad spirits as they lay untended.

The White Mountain stood no more, the Great Mountain had turned black with anger and the air was thick with the stench of battle!

Quickly Thunder Heart felt decieved as he envisioned the true cataclysm of the battle. He then heard the hollow of the crater began to roar again with life and fracture into splinters as the spirit's breaths again began to hiss from their darkened village beneath.

Thunder Heart's eyes quickly became withdrawn as he witnessed the valleys that rested far below the Great Mountain that he had spent his youth, as he then saw them rapt in smoke and desolate of life.

Large tongues of liquid fire rock spewed from the flanks of the mountain, great rivers of snow and mud had filled all the rivers and streams as far as he could see.

Thunder Heart then began to weep as he was heartbroken to have fought so gallantly only to admit that the battle was lost. Given his grief of losing the battle the ground beneath his feet exploded and sent his soul to the land's of his forefathers. The hot mud, water and fire rock from within the soul of the Bad Spirit then spilled down from upon the great mountain to the east and north, across the Great Water, and roared before the lands that lead to the peoples of the Klickitat.

Brave Heart's people were sullen by what they were witnessed. They determined that the Great Coyote Spirit had misled them as they were now surrounded by the fire rock and mudslides that were cast from high above the Great Mountain.

Brave Heart was heard to have warned his peoples of not believing the Great Coyote Spirit, and as he told his people of their wrongdoing the Great Coyote arrived from the east and commanded the floods to cease and all the people of Brave Hearts to be spared.

A few nights later, high up on the Great Fire Mountain, a new crater formed to hold the evil spirits, and they were then bound beneath to the fires of their villages as they danced before they could again attack the lands before them.

The Great Spirit, Coyote, then showed mercy and compassion on the grieving Brave Heart and his tribe, as he then promised them all the Sacred Lake and the surrounding lands to them so that they could again make their villages safe.

To those that chose to leave the lands beneath the Great Fire Mountain were then permitted to journey to the lands of the Wallowas and the Wahpoos Chuck, Snake River.

Elk Woman was granted her heart's desire as she was awarded her transformation into a solitary cone, and there she stands assuredly alone as the first and only Guardian of the Sacred Lake.

Knowing that Thunder Heart had been cruely decieved, the profile of the brave warrior was then sealed upon the face of the mighty Fire Mountain for all the suns and moons to pass.

The Lost Meadow Peoples
of Spirit Lake

Many suns and moons have passed since the days of the bad spirit's spells were cast between the great mountain spirits of Pahto and Wy-East

Otelagh, Sun, rose from behind the land's of the east, and the sun sat upon the great water's of the west with only the whispering of the winds crossing the trails of the lands.

It is these same suns and moons that have allowed the Spirit of the itchwoot, mowitch, moolack, and pish, Black Bear, deer, elk, and fish, to have thrived in great numbers across these appealing lands, and these same suns and moons favored our peoples as the mountains were rich with the, shot olallie, huckleberry.

We give thanks to the Hyas Tahmahnawis Tyee, Great

Spirit Chief, as he has allowed these gifts that are offered before us to replenish our strengths as our people's course across the spirit's inspiring grounds, and as the beasts spirit's hides grant us warmth through the Cole illahee's, winter's, frozen breaths.

Living amongst the land's of Loowit, the tribe of the Tupso Illahee Tillikum, Meadow People, were the favored children of Moon, and the daughter of Talupus, Coyote, who was the Great Spirit Chief to all life that gathered upon Earth.

The Meadow People were great hunters who's skills were well known throughout the mountain valleys that our tribe and the tribes of our brothers had taken refuge from the Skookum Tahmahnawis of Okoke Hyas Pishpish, Bad Spirit of the Cougar.

The peoples of the Meadow pleasured the Great Spirit as they weaved baskets that were scribed with tales of the Great White Mountains, and adorned with arrowheads that were honed from the shiny black glass shaped from the soul of the Great Mountains.

The hides our brother's wore were fashioned from the elk and deer, and with feather's of the Great Eagle. The Great Spirit promised that they would prosper upon these lands forever without fear of the bad spirit's truss.

Many brothers of separate tribes to the east and south would journey from lands that we have only heard through their stories as they too have passed through our lands, and they would trade in the shadow of the great basin along the banks of the eternal spring for meat and fruits, and this pleased the Great Spirit.

The Great Spirit's voice was one day heard to have stated to the peoples of all the mountain's valleys that; "I, Talupus, the Father Spirit of the Earth, has chosen the Meadow People to grace the lands resting below the princess, Loowit. I pledge that if they sacrifice their beliefs and find themselves lost by their own greed in taking of the animal spirits that run freely amongst us, that their souls shall forever find themselves favored by the Skookum Tahmahnawis of the Pishpish. If they do not abide by the laws that they now must accept, may the Skookum Tahmahnawis of the Klale Lolo take upon the side of the Skookum Tahmahnawis of the Pishpish and cast their soul's beneath the soils that you all now stand, and cast by the light of that day they shall quickly find themselves baited to the fiery chambers beneath Loowit for all the passing moons."

Upon accepting Coyote's words, Coyote bid Loowit, the princess of all the Great White Mountains, to become the guardian of these Meadow People.

As Loowit was then also pleased and tears fell from upon her gentle slopes, her tears then formed a beautiful saphire lake with trees alligning the shores that were gracefully spread beneath her feet, and where all the peoples of the lands would be welcomed to hunt and fish beneath the breadth of her peak.

Many days had passed and the life of the Meadow Peoples were found to be prosporous, and on a day when the spirits were pleased a medicine man journeyed before the great valley of Loowit, and here it was told that he stood upon a high ridge held high above the shores of the waters and peered from shore to shore as he chanted to the High Father Spirit.

This medicine man's name was Polaklie Skookum Noise Kopa Saghalie, Dark Thunder, as the tales tell of the Great Father's introduction upon Dark Thunder's final wail upon the high ridge.

Soon, the Meadow Peoples learned of the medicine man's powers to create wind as it was cast upon the lands, and it spread darkness upon the lands as mighty storms fell from the heavens as they journeyed from the east. The people feared Dark Thunder as they thought that he chose to cast a spell upon the warmth of day, and to punish all that lived beneath Loowit's rising peak with the breath of winter's Skookum Tahmahnawis.

Kumtux Leloo, Wise Wolf, the chief of the Meadow Peoples chose to dare the Spirit of Loowit and climb upon her untainted snow, and as the sun had crossed from the land's of the east and fell upon the west he prayed upon the Spirit of Loowit as he cried upon her flank;

"My guardian sister," he pleaded, "my peoples and yours have now fear implanted in our souls for the one that rests upon the high ridge named Dark Thunder. The maddened one who creates the winds and wishes these storms to cross our lands. I plead of you to give me the wisdom and strength to calm my people's hearts, and to allow them once again to be proven upon your winsome path."

Loowit quickly threw steam from her heights at her displeasure of Wise Wolf's trespass upon her slopes, and as she stood strong before his presence and fumed her displeasure, she began to scream from within the smoking crater below the dome of her summit.

"You foolish mortal! Do you think that I do not know of Dark Thunder and of his wish to bring the darkened clouds that hold rain that gives life upon the soils of these lands? Dark Thunder is to trace across all lands that the Great Father has treasured as his own, and you must know Dark Thunder is a messenger upon the trails of the Mighty Coyote."

Smoke and flame then spread from the crater upon Loowit's slope, and she began to exclaim her dismay towards Wise Wolf once again;

"You have dared to climb upon the sanctity of my slopes, and you leave deep fractures across my face! You have now scarred the untouched regions of my soul, and have found me bewildered to your trust before me! You have dared my soul to become heated by your thrust upon me, and now you must leave your best sacrifice before my crater, and then, and only then, shall I tell Sun of your concerns!"

As Wise Wolf stood faltering before Loowit's scold, he cautiously knelt before her and placed ten rare stones collected from many distant lands.

Then Wise Wolf quickly descended the snowy slopes that Loowit had challenged to be her own.

As Sun rose again from the east, Loowit scooped up the ten stones left by Wise Wolf and then began to speak to Sun; "Sun, Wise Wolf, the Chief of the Meadow People that live beneath my peak has told me of his people's complaint towards Dark Thunder. Wise Wolf has left before me ten stones as an offering for the trespass upon my virgin slope, and I ask you Sun, what must I answer him?"

Sun arched across the sky and watched the Meadow People as he crossed the trails that he chose, and before darkness fell upon the peoples of the Meadow, Sun spoke to Loowit; "Cast the stones into the lake before you, and when one moon has passed, all will know of the Great Spirit's will!"

So Loowit obeyed Sun, and as darkness fell across the lands, Loowit blew fire and smoke from above, and cast the ten stones into the lake's depths.

As the moon crossed the heavens, Loowit rumbled and cast from within her soul dark smoke and flame, and the Meodow People sat bewildered and shaken before the fire's of their counsel as they awaited Sun's response.

From the ridge that Dark Thunder chose to be his own, he sat and beat out his warning upon his drum, calling upon the Wind Spirits to quiet the sacred mountain and extinguish the fiery outbursts cast out by Loowit's embittered soul!

On the eve of the new moon ten White Deer Spirits were seen to arise from the waters of the sacred lake.

As fast as the eagle flies across the sky, Sun returned before Loowit and spoke from above her whitened robe; "The Father Spirit knows of your concerns! He has seen your promise upon his lands and grants peace and safety to all whom tread across the meadow's of Loowit's valleys."

Then Sun gave charge of the mysterious Deer Spirits to Loowit, and he challenged her to the urgency of their protection from all who did not know of their gifted spirit; "As long as you and the Meadow People obey the Saghalie Hyas Tahmahnawis, all life will be pleased upon your kingdom's floor!"

Loowit then asked of Sun; "Sun, what of Dark Thunder? What is the will of Coyote for him?"

Sun quickly replied; "Allow Dark Thunder to continue his battle songs, but do not allow him to leave his ridge. If he were to treasure below to the lands where your peoples find safety, he shall bring despair and suffering to all that live beneath your reign!"

And so it was for many suns that Dark Thunder sat lonely and quietly upon his distant ridge, and the Meadow Peoples lived in safety and prospered.

The Deer Spirits were revered by all for their High Spirit, and under the protection of Loowit, were given rich valleys to graze.

One day, after many suns had passed, Loowit was called from her mountaintop to attend a potlatch, meeting, of the Great Mountain Spirits. All the Great White Mountain's Spirits were to attend, the Great Tahoma, Loowit's suitors, the proud Wy-East and Pahto, and even the distant Kulshan, Mt. Baker, would be gathered together one last time.

Loowit rose up with pride as she was invited to visit with all the elder peaks, and sadly, she forgot to place a guardian overlooking the White Deer Spirits. Loowit also failed to place watch over Dark Thunder's station upon his ridge in her absence, and after many moons had passed, Dark Thunder came down from the ridge and entered the camp of the Meadow People.

The Meadow People had not seen Dark Thunder for many moons and did not notice that it was he that had escaped from his ridge and entered their village. Dark Thunder was very smart and had seen that the peoples would accept a stranger in their village if he were to offer gifts before them. He told Wise Wolf and his peoples that the presents were left by Loowit, and that he was chosen to offer these gifts to her favored peoples upon her visit before the tables of the potlatch.

Quickly, upon Dark Thunder's offering gifts, the Meadow People welcomed Dark Thunder and offered him lodging beside them, and they were then settled near the Sacred Lake.

Yet, Dark Thunder's heart was evil, and he soon became jealous of the Deer Spirits, and as Dark Thunder and a few young wariors sat before the fire of their camp, Dark Thunder was heard to chant; "You are mighty hunters, proud and brave! All the game is yours to take, even the deer of the Sacred Lake!"

As soon as Dark Thunder had cast upon the Meadow Peoples the first song he quickly began to cast a wicked spell upon the young warriors who knew that no harm should be placed upon the most honored Deer Spirits.

"Go forth and hunt them," chanted Dark Thunder.

"Show the tribes what mighty hunters you truly are!"

As the night grew long, Dark Thunder claimed upon the souls of the young warriors and sent them to the Valley of Many Streams, and it is known that the souls of the Deer Spirits were slain upon their beds beneath the sticks that gave shelter from the pishpish.

All but one!

Wounded, but still strong, the lone Deer Spirit ran to the shore of the Sacred Lake, and before entering the sacred waters, moaned to Wise Wolf and to the people of the village; "Your misguided youth have killed our spirits all! You have disobeyed the Great Father Spirit! May the heavens open and bring the storm upon your peoples, and may the winds cast your peoples far from Loowit's lands. May your eyes toil in tears and your hearts gather fear, as Loowit shall call upon Sun, and Sun shall seek those that disobey his promised word!"

With the final words spoken before Wise Wolf and his people, a green light was cast upon the water's of the Sacred Lake from the heavens, as are the fire rocks that chase their brothers across the heaven's trails as we sit before our campfires, and sadly, the only Deer Spirit to have survived the senseless slaughter, quietly fell into the moonlit waters and was never to have been seen again.

Swiftly, Loowit's towering form began to rumble and shake upon her return as she had heard tale of the young warriors hunt. Great fires were cast from her soul and fire rocks fell upon her shoulders! Loud screams and cries fell upon the ears of the Meadow Peoples from atop Loowit's smoldering peak, and in fear, the Meadow Peoples and Dark Thunder ran from the valley to escape the wrath of Loowit and fled to the River of the Wind.

For many days there was great smoke and flame that spread throughout the mountains and valleys of Loowit's range. The towering sticks that the forest was treasured were quickly felled and burned from upon their rich soils. Streams became rivers, and these waters coursed across the lands as mud, and this quickly smothered all life beneath its thickened wall.

In mortal fear of the High Spirits, Wise Wolf and his people sought out Dark Thunder and slew him before the spirits that were held high upon a distant mountain. The Meadow People chose to venture without regard for their error to the Ridge of Thunder below Loowit's smoking and burning fume, and it was there that Dark Thunder was buried beneath a rockfall high up on its western face.

The people's chose to offer only the coldness of sunsets and darkness to Dark Thunder's Spirit, and chose not for his soul to see the rising of the day's warmth again!

As the light of Sun rose across the sky, Sun again approached Loowit, and as he stood before her he scorned her as his voice resonated across all whom sat at the table of the potlatch. Sun was heard to explain; "The Meadow People have done great evil! Slain are the Mowitch Spirits, but one. Go back upon your peak quickly and see the error of your peoples, and witness to the error of your guard!"

Loowit fell from grace before all her brothers and sisters upon Sun's scorn. Loowit stood high up on the shoulders of her peak, and with tears flowing from her cheeks, she saw the beautiful forests she once cherished now flattened and burned.

All the Meadow Peoples had now vanished, and the Sacred Lake that flowed proudly beneath her ran red with the fallen Deer Spirit's blood.

But one!

As Loowit stood in disbelief, and as her spirit sank with the savageness of what now lay before her, Sun again appeared before her. As Loowit and Sun sadly peered across the ruins of what was once a much treasured land by all the Spirits of the Cascades, Sun slowly turned towards Loowit with a broken heart and stated; "This is the result of your foolishness! In your haste to sit beside your suitors you have failed the peoples and the Hyas Saghalie Tahmahnawis as you had not chosen for the Deer Spirits guard from Dark Thunder."

Loowit began to weep profusely as she hailed before Sun; "Oh Father, I have failed your word! Please bring back the trees and the Meadow Peoples, and I shall perform upon your every need!"

As Sun stood before Loowit and saw her agony, and as Sun had great fondness for Loowit as did Pahto and Wy-East, the Great Spirit solemnly spoke to her again; "The warriors of the Meadow People who has slain the Deer Spirits are now forever cursed! Let them dwell upon the bottom of the lake, and only at night are they allowed to be gathered as one unto their hunt!"

The Great Coyote then gave Loowit the punishment that she must concur towards the Meadow People, and with this, Coyote stated; "Your wisdom has been scarred, and now so shall your beauty be scarred before all your suitors within the Great White Mountain's Range!"

And at that, Coyote caused a large crevacce to form below Loowit's snowy crown.

Upon seeing the scar dwelt upon her once beautiful face, Loowit was quick to extend her wrath upon Wise Wolf and the Meadow People that lay hid beneath the peaks of the River to the Wind.

"You have done great evil and have betrayed me before Sun and the Great Father to the Earth," roared Loowit as she emitted smoke and fire rocks from the ugly scar that Coyote had created upon her features.

"You shall no longer enjoy the gifts that were once held to all the valleys and the waters. There shall be no fish or game to feed your peoples again! From this day forward the sun shall not bring warmth to the lands, and you shall not live as Meadow Peoples, but your likeness shall take on the shapes of beasts, and you will live high up amongst the cold breaths of winter, and where my frozen breaths shall linger forever within your souls!"

And so it was true from that day forward!

The water's of the lake and the river valleys were cursed from that day forward!

The Meadow People became hungry mountain beasts who found themselves descending Loowit's slopes once a new moon, and they would then steal peoples of different tribes who were foolish to venture near the shore of the Sacred Lake.

Upon the ridge that the wind blows as the sun and moon courses across the heavens, is now the home of the evil and scheming Dark Thunder. At night you can hear a ghostly howling from atop the ridge, and it is common to hear the howling before dark and sinister clouds form above the valley's darkened floor.

The sound of thunder echoes throughout the lands that Loowit now attentively guards with passion.

The young warriors that slew the Deer Spirits are now Demon Spirits that become unbound to their lair beneath the waters of the Sacred

Lake and hunt for the peoples that jest of their fate. The once young warriors now appear as mowitch and moolack, and lure the unwary visitor close to the water's edge. Then, they too, our lost brothers, shall not be seen again as they are then imprisoned to the Sacred Lake's darkened depths.

Tales of these young warriors of the Meadow Peoples soon spread far across the lands to our distant brothers, and to this day, our peoples avoid the Great Spirit Lake and our once beautiful maiden, Loowit.

The Legend of the White Salmon

My father and I sat before our campfire one warm summer's night
and he told that it was long ago when the Great Spirit Sun traveled
from the east to the west and overlooked the lands of Pahto as he
passed overhead. The Great Spirit had granted Pahto all the lands
divided between the Great Tehoma, and all the lands that were
separate from the kingdom of Princess Lawala Cloughs, and far
beyond to the Great River below.

Sun told Pahto, that as he passed above his lands upon the trail that
led his return to the lands of the east, that he must see below him the
lushness of the valleys upon his every pass, and he must lay witness
to the animal spirits as they graze freely within these same valleys, as
they would soon provide their souls upon their people's tables.

Many days and nights had passed since Sun spoke to Pahto, and
many of our fathers that had led our peoples had passed beyond to
the land's of the Great Spirits. Our fathers had become legends before
our tribe as they had led us safely upon the trail that granted our
survival before the Great Earth Spirit, Sun.

The legend is told that Sun had been pleased throughout his reign
above these majestic lands, but upon the darkest morning that he had
traveled above his claim to these lands, he witnessed a land now lain
ruined by Pahto's boiling storm.

The Great Spirit saw that far across the Great River and upon the
lands that Wy-East ruled had been challenged once again by Pahto
to claim the animal spirits that had been promised to Wy-East, as
they chose refuge beneath him and not within Pahto's own valleys.

Wy-East had sat silently for many moons upon his throne and guarded over his tribes and the beasts of the forests that lived below his silken robe.

Wy-East had awarded the peoples of the Chinook all the lands of his kingdom, and along all the rivers that were challenged with the Spirit of the Great Salmon, and upon the open plains that his people harvested food to survive the cold breaths that the bad spirit of winter had always promised to have accompany his return.

Sun peered down from the heavens and sorrowfully witnessed that Pahto had chose to open his vent once more and had begun to fire hot arrows and spears across the lands that lie to the south of his own, and as many fell short of their mark, the heat that was cast from Pahto's breaths had scorched all the trees and all the life that they once guarded beneath them.

Pahto's bad spirit had again forced all the animal spirits to flee, and his spirit had filled all the rivers and streams with silt that quickly swallowed all the fish spirits as they then lay hidden from the breath's of Sun that gives life to us all.

Pahto's kingdom was unmercifully swallowed by his own treachery and greed. The beautiful Lawala Clough who had once chosen Pahto to be her mate, sat in her beautiful gown high above her forested lands and witnessed the great terror that Pahto had chosen to swarm across all the lands beneath him.

As her heart then lay cold to Pahto, and her spirit fell from the heights of her kingdom in disbelief, she quickly swore upon herself to never journey before Pahto in attempt to sway his now heated and fuming soul.

The heavens were now thick with smoke as the lands were swept with fire, and all life that once were treasured upon them were not seen nor heard.

All sounds of life were quelled across all the Cascades for many seasons, from the north of the Great Tehoma, and to the south of the Great Waku-nunee-Tuki, Mt. Shasta, there fell silence across all the lands of the mighty tribe of the Cascades.

What had been once rich and flourishing kingdoms that the Great Spirits of the Cascades had been promised by the Hyas Sun Spirit now lay in ruin before them.

The soils upon what life had once flourished now were seen unkept, unwelcoming, and were held hostage by the Mesachie Tumtum of the Pishpish as it welcomed all who chose to cross the open plain below him as it now savored its next meal from upon its lofty perch.

Sun became angrier upon each pass of the lands beneath him, and it was the morning that the Great Spirits of the Cascades roared of their dismissal of Pahto that Sun passed overhead.

As Sun's eyes were quickly filled with tears and were surrendered forcefully from the heavens and fell upon the lands, a great flood settled upon the kingdom. From the mountains to the cliffs highest edge above the Great River, the water's depths soon challenged those of the Great River.

Many days had passed as the tears of the Great Spirit fell upon the kingdom of Pahto, and as the heavens remained dark and gray, and were tethered taut with the stench from the fires that had then burnt the soul of the land, our peoples had lost their way upon the trails that we had once followed our great leaders away from evil.

Our ancestors were surrendered to the lands that they were then joined, and they had lost their way due the evilness of Pahto's Mesachie Tumtum as the remaining light to be cast before them were lit from the lances cast from the Great Thunder Spirits as they speared across the plains before them.

The peoples of our tribe that once praised the Great Spirit now stood confused as Sun stood opposed to their return within the safety of their villages.

Our drums could be heard throughout our nation undisturbed as their rhythm spelled of their plight, and as the cadence of the drum beats told of their plead before the Great Earth Spirit through the silence of the darkened night's hold, and the rhythm of our brother's drums spread throughout all the lands surrounding those that they were then imprisoned.

The Great Earth Spirit slowly crossed the heaven's trail above the lands that were once rich with life, and upon his pass above their horizon he thought that he must desist from allowing them to return within Pahto's kingdom. He chose instead to punish Pahto, and he had decided that Pahto had chosen to allow his kingdom to become immersed in fire and then swallowed by flood, and was soon to lie in ruin as the soils that once held together the spirit of his kingdom were to be immersed and veiled by clay, that he should stand alone and wail before all the spirits of the Cascades as his soul had again fallen submissive before them through his abandonment of their trust.

It is told that the water's of the great flood were held to the lands of Pahto and did not fall to the Great River, and that all life, animal, the great forests, and our peoples, were all led away from the lands that they had chose to live.

Pahto became detached and yearned for the companionship of his brothers that he could see thrive around him, and as the Great Earth Spirit passed over his lands, Pahto slowly became defeated and fell silent once more.

Each morning Sun passed overhead Pahto, and as he leeringly peered down upon the loss of his kingdom, Sun saw Pahto sitting as does a stone upon the ground, alone, yet surrounded by his own brother's villages.

The Great Earth Spirit saw that Pahto had lain his flattened head low before all his brothers and sisters of the Cascades, and it was upon a day long since past of Pahto's ruin of his kingdom that Sun's passed overhead and once again chose to challenge Pahto.

"Raise your face again to the east when I arrive upon the horizon, and as you look for my entrance into these lands, you shall know that the time has arrived for you to denounce the demon spirit that you hold within your soul. You shall offer Wy-East whatever he asks for your trespass into his kingdom, and you shall abide by his wishes as he now holds the power to take whatever he chooses from what was once treasured within your purse.

It has not been long since the battle you held with Wy-East in the past, and that you had been requested to give half of all your peoples and animal spirits to his kingdom. This day may leave you without all that you had once tightly grasped to your kingdom, so beware what you say before him."

As Sun's lecture was completed before Pahto, Pahto sat silent and questioned his value before all the spirits of the Cascades. He thought of all the harm he had brought forth his brothers and sisters, and with great sorrow, he quickly lowered his eyes from the tower of his own brother's and sister's peaks and began to chant a promise to

Wy-East that was heard throughout all the kingdoms that reigned from the Great Waters of the west, to the Great Mountains of the east, to the Spirited Shasta to the south, and to the villages north where our families once journeyed through as we were soon to discover the Lands of Wah along the Hyas Columbia.

"My brother, Wy-East! I have fallen from the graces of the Great Spirit once again, and as my spirit has given reign to the bad spirit that arises from within my soul, I have caused great harm to fall across all the lands that are separated by the Great River between us. I plead that you hear my words as they fall from the heavens above and lie stationed before your feet. I plead that you will not dismiss my invitation to become one with the Great Earth Spirit once again.

I do not ask for my people's return, nor do I plead for the animal spirits to again run free across my lands. I have sat upon the crown of my own spirit, and as I sat unwelcomed before all my brothers and sisters of these lands that we have been promised, I have not seen your eyes turn towards my kingdom, not once.

Many moons have crossed above the heavens as my crown has been covered with the blackened soul of the beast within me. The same beast that I promise before you that shall now flee from my soul and never return to these lands that we rise above.

This beast shall flee from my soul and follow the trails that lead to the Great Waters, and it shall be seen no more.

I accept the challenge that Sun has asked of me to expel the anger of the Bad Spirit from my soul and cast it across the trails that fall below the heights of my lands. I ask you not to return what I hold valuable within my soul until I have proven that my spirit has again evolved into what Sun had chosen for me.

I plead that you do not dismiss my thoughts as those of the Mesachie Tahmahnawis, but that you stand upon your crown and witness the spirit thatlies within me as it flees to the depths of the Great River and never again to return.

I shall promise that as the bad spirit flees from my soul, a great channel shall open upon the lands that will allow the waters that Sun had once wept long ago to fall into the Great River, and that a Great White Salmon shall one day find its tribe thick with promise as they gather beneath the water's fall, and he shall lead his tribe to the waters that form beneath me.

As the Great White Salmon Spirit leads his tribe before these lands, the animal spirits and my peoples shall return upon their own approval, and you shall also witness that my spirit has once again evolved into the Kloshe Tumtum that all my brothers and sisters had not envisioned me to stray.

I plead before you Wy-East, do not fear the smoke that shall soon rise above me, as this shall be the last that all my brothers and sisters of our tribe shall witness of the bad spirit's claim to the kingdom that Sun had promised me to safely rule."

Many days passed and Wy-East stood in silence to Pahto's promise. The breaths of winter's frozen spirit rose and fell across all the lands, and Pahto sat once again upon his peak in silence, without knowing if he were to be allowed again within the summit's of their potlatch.

The Great Earth Spirit passed overhead and saw that Pahto sat in silence and had once again found fortitude within himself, and upon witness to Pahto's patience, he spoke to Pahto and shared the approval spoken of Wy-East to his plead before him.

Pahto upon hearing the words spoken of Wy-East gathered his strength and chanted unto the Kloshe Tumtum to guard him from the Mesachie Tumtum's soul, and he then released the bad spirit to dwell deep within the depths of the water's of the Great River below.

A great wall of molten rock was sent down upon the lands to the Great River, and from this rock's fire was cast a great channel that then held the tears of Sun to chase the bad spirit from the land.

For many seasons the waters had filled all the lands as the Great Earth Spirit wept as he passed overhead and peered down upon the blackened and unkept lands beneath him.

As the bad spirit fled the soul of Pahto, Sun, upon his passing above Pahto's kingdom, gave to the land the gift of warmth once more and allowed the grasses and trees, and the flowers and huckleberry to rekindle their affairs upon them.

The waters were deep and took many moons to fall beneath to the Great River, and soon they too were promised to challenge the tides of the distant Salt Chuck.

As the Great Earth Spirit passed overhead the kingdom's of Pahto and Wy-East, the return of life brought pride once again to the kingdoms of their rule.

The trees grew strong and reached far into the heavens, and the grasses grew thick and waived in the Great Spirit's calming breaths. The kloshe tupso stretched as far as the Great Spirit could see as they brought color and sweet scent to the land, and the huckleberry grew thick in the open meadows upon Pahto's side, and they were then lain in promise once again to the peoples upon their return.

As the spirit of winter passed and the spirit of spring arrived, there were great numbers of salmon that were seen as our tribe was challenged by the fast waters of the Great River. The salmon were told to be many as our peoples had stepped upon their backs and crossed the fast waters of the Great River to the gates before the Council of Wahclella and beneath the fall of the Great Multnomah.

The salmon spirits gathered beneath the water's fall at the base to the river that would lead them to the lands below Pahto. As their numbers grew, rising from beneath the deep waters of the Great River arose the Hyas Tumtum of the Tkope Salmon.

Strong and proud he appeared as he leapt from beneath the water's fervent rush, and it was here, beneath the water's fall that had once chased the bad spirit from the lands, that the Great White Salmon began to lead his tribe to the safe waters in the kingdom that Pahto now rules peacefully above.

Sun had crossed the heavens and smiled upon all the lands of the Cascades, and as he soared above the lands of Pahto he saw below that the eena, klale lolo, moolack, mowitch, and all the animals and birds that had fled had chosen to follow the Hyas Tkope Salmon into Pahto's kingdom and returned to the land of their own villages.

It is told that the Great Tkope Salmon may be seen on the night of the full moon, as it is upon the light of the moon that a bright light shines across its back as it leads its tribe from beneath the waters of the Great Salt Chuck, and points them along the channels held deep within the Great River to the waters that are now promised to gently fall from the heights of Pahto's silenced rule . . .

Chapter 1
The Council

Klahowya!

This evening, my father, the great Chief to our peoples, Two Spirits, Mokst Tahmahnawis and I, Land Otter,

Nenamooks, after feasting on salmon that we have caught in the creek belonging to the Eagle, are found resting before the campfire, and my father has begun to tell the tale of our beginnings within the Land's of Wah.

For many years of my youth my father had shared stories of our peoples as we have lived within these lands where we are established today. I have heard how the salmon were treasured in the Valley of the Eagle as they gathered in great numbers across the fast waters of the Great River. I have always known that our peoples for many seasons walked upon the trails of these lands, and that our tribe, part of the great Chinook Nation, had been blessed by the spirits of this mighty river and by the mighty peaks that we, the Watlallas, are surrounded.

Our peoples have built shelters and longhouses to keep us warm in the winter's frozen breaths along the river's course to the western sea, and to this day, our peoples live near the Great Chute where it can be seen that the Salmon gather tightly below the falls as they await their turn to leap far from the water's plane upon their long journeys home.

I patiently sat warming myself by our fire as my father told the stories that his father and his father before him had shared with the youth that sat upon these very grounds before proceeding upon their visioned quests before the spirits that are held honorable to the mighty tumwatas that descend from the mighty peaks of these Cascades.

The stories that my father has allowed for my consideration were well chosen as I was to begin my own trek amongst these majestic lands in hope to become a shaman before my tribe's peoples. Through the wisdom that these spirits may share before me if I am allowed to further upon the trails of my quest as their truths are spelled upon me, shall keep our souls safe and far from the grasp of the bad spirits that hide amongst us.

I must listen to each and every word that my father shares and not fail my passage before the high spirits that have ruled these lands from our peoples ariival upon them.

I am awed by the tales that my father shares as I have asked him of our heritage for many years to what bond we had at first been honored to this most amazing country, and this night, he has explained to all my questions.

My father's eyes gave proof that his pride still stood stoically upon its own measure as he spoke of the pestilence that our tribe's ancient and most auspicious past has revealed.

The stories that our great chief shared extended for many hours this evening as we sat listening and enthralled to each and every word of his speech.

As we sat before the fire of our potlatch as darkness fell upon us we could hear the call of the coyote upon the Chinook winds, and as time passed quickly we soon discovered the rising of the sun over the crowns of the great cedars that stood surrounding our encampment.

My father's voice reminded me of the thunderous clap of the spirits that are held to their village high above us as their roars follow the long fingers of their hands as they streak across the heaven's skies and bring light to the darkest of the nights!

Before this eventful evening my father had not spoken endlessly of our ancestors, but this evening was not like any other that we had shared. The rythym of our peoples upon these magnificent lands were as clear as the full moon, and this night it is so named the Advance-in-a—Body-Moon.

My great leader spoke of the many tumwaters that speak within these magical lands as they draw down the healing waters unto us. He explained how they cleanse our souls from the Evil Spirits that are known to loom in every movement of our lives.

He also spoke of how the Spirit's of these Cascades promised our ascension unto the heavens once we are found acceptable before them as we follow in their ways and share their lessons to all that pass upon the trails that we share.

My father further explained the significance of the treasures held within the bowl of our Goddess, Metlako.

He exclaimed that Metlako was honorably chosen to become witnessing before all peoples that gathered before her as she shared of the mighty pish's fight to safely return to their homewaters beneath her, and as her story has been told and retold for many moons she has become a legend and is known today as the Goddess of Salmon.

I have come to understand by my many ventures before Metlako that she has affirmed her station rightly before the entrance to the Valley of the Eagle as her treasures lie peacefully and protected beneath her covering cliff.

It is here, at the entrance to her lands, that we, the sons of our fathers, are now joined in our potlatch.

As we sit about the fire and listen to our leaders speak of the trials that would soon challenge us, we are quickly overwhelmed by their offers in our guidance to succeed before the Hyas Spirits that we shall soon be standing before their judgment of our worth as leaders before our tribes.

The objective of our travels we are to believe is to search for the feather belonging to the great eagles that soar throughout our lands.

Our fathers, the braves and chiefs of our peoples, speak to our trial of manhood that lies pleasingly before us. The same trial as they had once undertaken before the spirits that surround us throughout the days and nights of our lives.

In answer to our questions about these trials we are soon to encounter, the fathers and chiefs of our tribes cast our questions aside from the Valley of the Eagle's test. We are told only that the High Spirits would be displeased if they were to share their knowledge of their own test and passage into the spirit world before we found ourselves challenged across the lands that hold tightly to our fates.

My father stands before us as he speaks of the lands chosen of the lolo, the bear; "These lands, are not to be entered if the Great Metlako is not assured of your worthiness before her as her test shall share of your own mettle and wisdom before her trial. Your presence upon the Land's of the Lolo, and before all the lands of Wy-East must be warranted by each of our forefathers that clinch tightly to the allowance of your passing. Metlako holds within her purse the authority to allow you to either pass further to the sanctuary of the Lolo, or your dismissal before the spirits that reign hardened upon the trail that proves your soul yet unfledged from their way.

By this first lesson, you must first earn the honor before Metlako, and only then shall you be entitled entrance upon the honorable land's of the Lolo that lie beyond the trail's turn ahead."

My father speaks of great meadows reaching beyond the borders of the Valley of the Eagle as the lands of our creator are spread further than his eyes can see.

He shares tales of the many rivers that lead into the Valley of the Eagle, and warns that each holds within its treasure an announcement cast by its Spirit as to their significance to the lands that they are held.

My father also states the Spirits will award their wisdom only if we are found responsive to the High Spirit's words.

My father tells of these river's maddened swells as they are cast by the melting winter snows of our Great Spirit, Wy-East.

There are stories of moolack that gather upon the forest's floor as they are found descending upon these meadows as great storms rise up from above the meadows of Wy-East's throne.

My father exclaims that he proposes that these moolack gather in great numbers within the Valley of the Eagle as they fight to survive the savagery of the frozen breaths and deep snows promised by the Cole Illahee's Bad Spirit upon the Land's of the Lolo's frozen heights.

My father tells to the story of how one day given a hunt for the mighty Moolack that had chosen to his name before our peoples.

As I look towards my father as his voice resonates within me, he stands before the fire with the flicker of the flame glowing upon his face, and it is then that I sense for the first time the stature that he solidly holds before our people!

My father stands proudly as he proclaims that it was during a hunt that he approached the moolack upon an open meadow that he had acquired and was rewarded the name, Mokst Tahmanawis.

Throughout the stories unfolding my father extends his words into a dance as it is shadowed by the blaze of the fire.

My father slowly weaves the story of the hunting party's approach towards the great herd through the trees, as the moolack, with unfearing souls, stood silently and stilled to their approach before them.

Just as he had arisen before the moolacks that memorable morning and as they stood unalarmed by the hunter's presence, he arose silently before us.

As my father stood from behind a stick's cover he quickly enacted the deadly and pointed shot from his bow upon the neck of not one, but of two impressive bulls.

The arrowhead that he had fashioned from the black glass that we trade with our brothers from the east sent both moolack upon all our tables that night.

I now understand the honor of the great robe that my father gathers onto his broadened shoulders as his robe holds not one, but two hides given by these moolack's fallen spirits.

As my father speaks throughout the moon's rise and fall of this night, his thoughts have kept me drawn to his stories into the rising of the sun. I have caught my thoughts drifting upon the paths that are soon to lead me through the lessons that will guide my life. and I am yet to envision the trials that lie in wait before me as they are chosen by the Saghalie Tyee Tahmahnawis, God Spirit.

As I have sat here and listened to my father I have allowed my curiosity to wander beyond what his words have chosen for me to learn, and I know I must be ready to attach myself completely to *any and all of the lessons granted by the Great Spirits chosen of this valley. I must remind myself to stay attentive to every passing moment as the Spirits may call upon my name, and I must be attentive to answer their every call.*

As this day has been wanting by all those that gather around our fire, the group of our father's sons anticipate our recruitment in one day becoming leaders of our peoples.

We, the sons of our fathers that are chosen of these lands are impatient before the Great Spirits that speak nobly amongst the tumwaters of these lands!

My senses share that we have readily accepted whatever these trials may deliver, so that we may become as honored before our people as has our fathers before us.

The chiefs of all the Cascade's tribes have chosen us, and they have taken their turn in explaining how our efforts may lead us before the legendary spirits ruling the Valley of the Eagle and the Land's of Wah.

Once again, the great chief of our people, my father, has arisen upon the podium of these grounds to speak to the Tahmahnawis of Okoke Koosagh, the Spirit's of the Sky.

"Cast within the eyes of our sons, the sons of warriors and the sons of chiefs of our tribes beneath these Cascades, seen high above our lowly human forms, soaring above the prestigious Columbia, wrought by the Great Missoula, exists the magnificent, the Tahmahnawis' of Okoke Koosagh.

My sons, you now stand before the most powerful of the Bird Spirits belonging to the heavens. They, who soar upon the highest winds above the Valley of the Eagle are honored by gifts offered from within the water's of Metlako. The mightiest of these land's eagles shall be found perching upon the tallest sticks, trees belonging to Metlako in the valley of her choosing.

It is upon these spellbound grounds that you shall know the teachings given by the most highly revered of all their heralding spirits.

As you enter upon the likeness of the tumwaters as they gracefully fall before you, you shall encounter the Great Okoke Koosagh that shall persuade your unfledged souls to banish from your spirit your young and foolish ways.

"You are now hereby released to the patience and wisdom belonging to the deities of our past.

Accept the discipline of this charge, and you shall be entitled one day to be leaders before the brothers and sisters of our villages.

Young Warriors!

Begin your journey toward manhood as the Great Spirits belonging to the Valley of the Eagle beckon you forward."

Upon completion of my father's speech all of our teachers began to beat upon the great drums as they announced the beginning of our trials to the village's of our nation.

As the rhythm of their stamp rushed toward the avenues of Sun, our fathers began to chant to the Hyas Spirits for our safe challenge within the forest's shadows to begin.

As the drums rode the winds through the Valley of the Eagle, we, the children of our tribes holding to the Great Chinook threw our strengths upon the Cascade's cliff.

Climbing steadily along the trail carved from the face of the high rock we swiftly sought our destiny of becoming shamans unto all those that may one day look towards us for their delivery to the gates of the Hyas Tahmahnawis.

Chapter 2
Metlako

Fastened to the course of the trail that leads us higher from the water's lap far beneath us, we each begin our journey as we strive forward to reach the heralded Feather of the Eagle that awaits our arrival above Metlako's gracefull falls.

As my time arrives and I depart from alongside the fires of our camp, I turn to my father and nod before him as I am earnest to please him, as well to prove my own worthiness before our most heralded spirits.

With each stride I climb higher along the trail's ledge, and from the heights of the trail are offered views into this magnificent valley.

With their frozen silken robes the high peaks of the Cascades stand proudly from across the river that now lies far behind me, and their presence offers me strength as I pass the many tall sticks, trees, that stretch far into the heavens, and the great Cedar that line the trail's edge offers my senses to its sweet scent. As I pass beside the kloshe tupso, wildflowers, rising up from the rich soils to touch my soul, their many hues take my thoughts from the steep rise of the trail and soften my tread across the rocky path as I pass beside them.

I know I am entering into a land chosen sacred by our Great Sun Spirit, Otelagh, and this valley is told to be the home of many of our father's spirits that once reigned before our peoples. It shall be these same spirits that shall allow my passage beyond the measure of their trial, and it is before each and every of these trials that I believe I am to be held independent above all my brothers that will allow my passage unto the grottoes before each successive Tumwater, waterfall, thereafter.

My dream alike my fathers is to reach the highest pinnacle we mortals can obtain. To stand above all the land's of Wah at the Great Larch, Larch Mountain, and understand that we are one with our people's spirits, and to be able to see through our union, we shall all prosper and live on so others may follow in our footsteps and be gathered alongside these great walls that now rise to the great river that lead our canoes upon the course of the setting sun and to our distant brother's villages.

As my thoughts return upon the trail's lead I have now touched upon its flattened course as I am quickly announced to its thunderous roar as the Creek of the Eagle races unchecked from its birth from high above Metlako's cliff.

As I reach the edge of the cliff that separates the Eagle's distant banks from one another, held as promised by our fathers, are great numbers of our most heralded Chakchak, Eagle, Spirits. With strength attached to their golden talons and sharpened beaks, and honored with the innocence of their whitened heads and tails, they scream incessantly upon their disturbance by my arrival before them.

As I peer beneath their clutch to the mighty firs that they are gathered above the bowl of Metlako I can see many pish, salmon, flashing in the water's pool. It is here, within the flattened sanding bed of the Eagle's Creek that our salmon surrender their souls so that the young of their families may one day follow in their traces and return to these same waters, and in their return, they shall offer hope in that their brotherhood's survival rests upon the stealth beneath the darkened depths where pretends the Mesahchie Tahmahnawis', Bad Spirit's kingdom.

Our people's own survival rests upon the return of the salmon to our great river as they pass before our nets, and it is then that their *spirits offer our own survival amongst the Cole Winds, cold breaths, of our long winters.*

My father told me one day long, long ago that we should always honor the purity of all the waters that pass through our kingdom, and that we must never attempt to change the course of any river or creek as it passes across our lands.

My father continued to share that once waters were claimed behind walls built by the Eena, beaver, disease fell across our kingdom and many of our brothers fell hurriedly from their step upon these lands.

I now stand before the gracefulness of Metlako's fall and understand further why she is named as the queen of all the tumwaters that spill into the great river. It is not her great heights that have honored her with the crown, but it is her power as she protects the Pish's spirits arrival given each season that they return to her creek.

With a rush of cold wind from high above where I stand has settled a lone Eagle upon a branch anchored upon the cliff's face between myself and the creek far below.

I am honored as I stand here and am able to stand close to our most heralded of the Bird Spirits. I remember the lesson that I am to accept in the capture of the elusive Great Eagle's Feather, but as I stare intently into its piercing eyes my heart begins to race. I sense that if I dare reach out and thrust my weight toward this great chakchak, I shall fall quickly to my death, and in doing so, I shall fail in my father's wishes, and of my own.

"I dare not!" I say silently to myself.

I fall to my knees in search for guidance from the High Spirits as I am unsure to what I should do, and once my wail before them is cast soundly to the heavens, is heard in answer a voice that settles my soul as I was certain to fail upon my quest.

"Nenamooks, it is here before Metlako that you have first shown promise in that one day you may lead safely your peoples from harm as you accept your own mortality, and seek guidance from those before you who stood where you now stand. It is not the eagle's feather that you shall seek from this day forward, but your trial now rests in your understanding and acceptance of all the trials and lessons that you will encounter along the trails within these lands and all the lands where your trail lies before you.

With the wisdom borne within you from your father and his father before him we grant you passage to follow your heart, and to offer your soul to our wishes.

"This, we the spirits that hold honorable to the likeness of the Hyas Chakchak now grant you to further upon your dream."

"You may pass further towards the Lands of the Lolo that lie distant far above where we now stand, and may your journey be found worthy by all our trust."

My time has not been wasted as I stand before Metlako's presence and think back to the lessons my father had once shared before me. But it is now time that I follow the wise words spoken by the Spirit of the Chakchak and deliver my strengths upon those lands that are held to the Klale Lolo, Black Bear.

Chapter 3
The Cry of the Pishpish

As I walk along the Trail of the Eagle I have visions of a story my grandfather once shared of the Pishpish' ambush from the high rocks above this trail that took many of our brothers far from the villages of our ancestors as they allowed their trust and their lead by the chief to fail them.

It was a story that began like most other days, just as this day too has shone promise upon us all, but there was one difference that brought sadness to that day, as all those of our tribe that chose their travel upon this path were lost to the shadowy cast of the great pishpish and its shrieking dirge.

This is the tale that is shared by our great chief, and my father, as the story has been tuned to the children's ears of our tribe each night that we have shared the fire alongside him, and they ask for him to fill their young ears with many tales involving the golden cat of our lands.

This tale has been told amongst our peoples from the beginnings of our forefathers, and still to this day its truths are surrendered deeply amongst our beliefs.

I was just a boy when my father first sat before a fire one summer's evening and spoke of a pishpish that was gathered along the cliffs above the trail.

As I stand upon the very site of our brother's mistrust of the Hyas Chief's questioning, I can recall the words that my father spoke to the Hyas Tahmahnawis as he repeated his father's words and plead for our lost brother's safe return from their gathering of the great huckleberry.

"Our people stand before you as the Great Owl flies through the silence of the moon's journey across the heaven's of the Great Earth, we implore to you, our Great Spirit.

We appeal to your powers in order that you shall allow the safe return of our brothers that have chosen the wrong trail in their approach towards our door.

We seek the Kokostick, Woodpecker, Spirits to drum upon the body of the trees that stand above our brothers, and allow them to select the path that is lit by your guidance that shall allow their lives to be spared.

May the Crow spread its wings over them and lead them safely once again to the trail that offers their souls to again find faith in our leader's direction.

If they are protected from the great Puma we know the spirits of the forest shall have led our brothers to the encompassing of our fires.

As the wise owl booms his resignation from the trees above our gathering we appeal to your wisdom!

May the powers of your Spirit bring light to the trail's darkness, and may our brothers be once more found safe before our fires.

As dusk is now owned by the surrendering sun we alarmingly shout!"

Many long summer nights I have had to take on the face of the stealthy hunter that inhabits these lands. As this story tells of our ancestors' lack of faith in the chief of their village and his understanding to the lesson that the Hyas Tahmahnawis had chose for them that day is to be remembered as The Polaklie of okoke Pishpish, The Night of the Cougar!

As many of our tribe were returning from the Valley of the Eagle and were walking beside the majestic waters of Metlako they were suddenly seized by the Pishpish's grievous Spirit.

I recall that my father asked the young children of our camp to be attentive toward his words and allow their eyes to close so that their imagination can take seed in order that they may see within their souls the great golden pishpish luring them toward her lair.

My father wished for the children to see the pishpish's majestic and shadowy trace so that they too should become aware of the Mesahchie Spirit, Bad Spirit, that inhabits her unkindly soul.

He told them of the many nights that our brothers sat about the campfires, and of the mighty pishpish as her challenging shrill told of her ghastly stroll amongst us.

As I too recall the story I grow cold and found myself looking into the darkness of night, and anxiously awaited the pishpish's cry that can be heard throughout these lands!

The sun had long past below the horizon of the Cascades and as the moon began its climb from behind Wy-East, arising upon the evening's air, a rousing and horrendous scream was heard.

The screech of the great cat was captured in all the valleys surrounding the trail along the Eagle, and not a man nor woman of our tribe could discern its charge.

It was soon determined that our tribe was surrounded by the elusive Spirit of the Pishpish!

I remember amusingly as many of the children stirred before the fire at the thought of the Pishpish surrounding their path, and just as the hoot of a kwel kwel, large owl, filled the silence of the stilled air surrounding our camp's fire, and with a shriek of their own, the youngest children of our camp were quick to cling to their mother's breasts.

The arrival of the Great Horned Owl above our fire could not have been better timed into the scene of the Hyas Pishpish's screaming cry!

Uncertain to what direction our tribe should flee to evade the chants of the Pishpish, our peoples were indeed lost.

Knowing that the Pishpish left no tracks along the trails of their hunt and were known only to leave the remains of their prey, must have created fear in the heart's of our brothers and sisters as they felt their lives were now in question and their spirits may soon be consumed by the great pishpish.

Our tribe's members fearfully gathered near one another while questioning their chief for guidance.

As the chief stood silent and petitioned the Hyas Spirits for their lead, he was immediately answered, and wisely told his peoples that the path of safe return would be the trail leading to the great river that they had earlier traveled.

As the chief finished recanting the words spoken to him by the Spirits another rousing scream nearer than the one before arose before them. In that moment, all were confused and unable to accept the chief's council as they were hopelessly surrendered to the Pishpish's petition for its next meal.

It is here where I now stand that the Cat Spirit had chosen to lie in ambush, hidden by the darkness of the forest's uncaring soul.

Sadly, the members of our tribe had chose to disobey the Hyas Spirits and their souls were then ambushed and suppressed within the sharp teeth of the PishPish.

As the chief stood angered by their foolish choice, the mortal screams of his remaining tribe could be mournfully heard as the Pishpish consumed their distrusting and calloused souls.

I am well versed in this story's truths, I believe that if we are one day chosen to be judged for our faith in the Great Spirits, we must not allow our judgment to deny the order of the Hyas Tyee. But we must ask our Spirit's guidance so that we may be mercifully led.

As there are many Spirits that lead us to success, we must not question their existence or we may quickly be served upon the table before this same PishPish Spirit.

We must find respect and exhibit honor before the spirits that watch over our disconcerting lives, and we must always believe and accept their wise words as they have led our peoples safely through many difficulties as these obstacles have confronted us all in our lives . . .

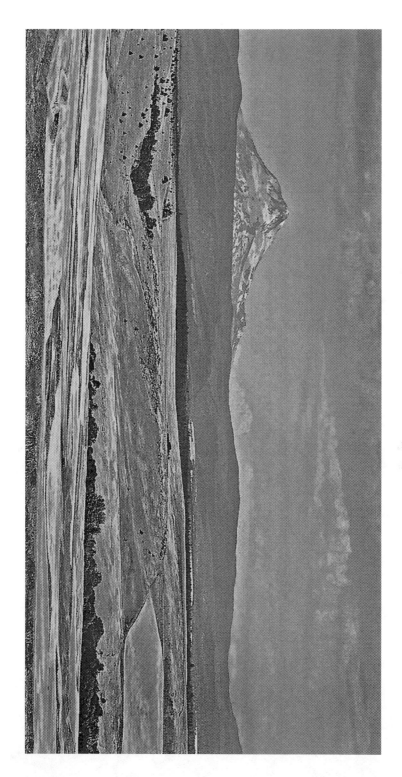

Chapter 4
Kokostick

I have traveled through many meadows, their flowing plains of golden grasses and radiant flowers directing my course to the Spirit of Wy-East. I have seen scarce signs of life fronting my path across these meadows, and as I approach the crest of a grassy knoll I find standing before me a solitary tree rising above the cover of the clouds.

It is within this tree that I hear the timely pounding of a kokostick as it beats upon the prow of its hollow drum.

Slowly as I enter upon the grounds of this bird's stage and extend my sights toward the higher reaches of this stick's extending branch, I spot the red crested drummer tapping upon the very facing of this swaying tree.

This drummer's rhythym was meant for my consideration as its toll rode upon the winds of the Great Chinook, as many kokostick's songs are sung. Yet I stand mystified as its beat registers little response within my soul!

I am certainly questioned by the spirit's lesson along my journey through this meadow.

I silently stand beneath this kokostick's fasten upon the stick that it has merged, and through the uncertainty of my thoughts, I stand challenged.

As this kokostick's drumming begins to take charge of my heart's own rhythmic beat, I throw off my wariness and I am soon engulfed by the qualities that the Hyas Tahmahnawis had earlier pledged.

My own spirit rises as if it were attached upon the winds of the Great Chinook. My sight extends toward the heights that this Kokostick has chosen to perform, and I hear the Kokostick's beliefs to my own journey as if it were now spoken by my own tongue.

"By the wishes of the Hyas Wy-East I now stand upon the limb of this stick and spread upon the breaths of the Great Chinook the lesson that you shall carry throughout all the lands.

You must remain pointed to your vision Nenamooks, as you are the eldest son to Mokst Tahmahnawis.

Sit beneath the great tree of knowledge that we now share and hear the voices of the great Kulakula Spirits as they now fly into your soul. For they shall teach their lesson in the pulse of my rhythmical poll.

By the decoration of the first feather placed upon our wing our Spirits were honorably cast upon the avenues of the winds, and accepted before Sun's review. Challenged by the heaven's breaths we have been chosen to soar to the lands unbeknownst by the tribes of your nation

Our Spirits have been praised as we have conquered the valleys of the Earth's most heralding peaks, and our spirits have in turn honored these rising sticks that bond with the soils of our earth.

As the sticks choose to grant their support upon the lands that we fly beneath, you must determine their survival announces that the seeds that have been cast from the heaven's breaths that are watered by the tears shed by the Hyas Illahee Tahmahnawis have given honor to these giants as they are necessary to our survival.

You must relate to your brothers that live upon the lands that the forests give life to all, as their union of heaven and earth breathes life to all that thrive above, within, and beneath the sanctuary of their cover.

You must respect the sticks that thrive within the forests, and as you gather those spirits for your needs, and to warm your shelters through the chilling breaths of winter's Mesahchie Tahmahnawis, Bad Spirit, you must be cautious to the number that you sacrifice.

You must place trust in your brother's beliefs that their own ascension to the heavens may one day be found by the branching paths that these very sticks may lead!

I sit and listen to the drummer's last fading tap upon this stick's prow, I remember a walk that my father and grandfather and I once took through the Talon's of the Eagle. We had set ourselves upon the trail of the Great Eagle, just as I am journeying today. As we were approaching a glade beneath a hillside's rise I noticed that all the life that we had earlier encountered through the corridor of trees had now long disappeared.

I grew curious to why their numbers were not welcomed upon the openness of this field as the sun chose to cast its warm and untethered rays upon its face.

My grandfather spoke of the day that our tribe chose this very meadow that had once been tightly filled with stands of cedar.

These sticks were quickly formed into the very canoes that we hold upon the shores of the Columbia near our village today.

My grandfather told me of the danger that life may encounter as bad spirits now hide in the darkness that encircles this defenseless meadow.

He reminded me that it is here that the great Pishpish awaits the moolack and mowitch that travel along this meadow's barren course.

I recall my sudden turn at that given moment toward the forest's enclosure certain that I had seen the shadow of a pishpish as it's toothy smile was directed at my path, and I was assured that I was promised to be its next meal.

I also recall my grandfather and father roaring with laughter over my swift feet as the dust that arose was quickly spread to the heavens behind me.

In this one encounter, I have promised myself to honor the Hyas Saghalie Tyee's castle and not be found within the toothy smile and fattened belly of a famished pishpish as it lies in wait along the borders of the forest.

Chapter 5
The Spirit Of Great Cedar's Soul

I must be cautious as I savor the treasures that lie hidden upon my journey. I must remain open to my thoughts of my quest as I am my father's hope to become the leader of our village, just as he was once chosen to test his mettle by these very trials that I find myself challenged.

The grounds that glisten along my journey retain the delicacy of the butterfly, and I must not close my heart to all that it offers. As I walk amongst the footsteps of all those before me that were also chosen to this trek, I must discover the treasures that hide before me. In these treasures hold my challenge, and in these same challenges offer our beliefs and pledges that we have honored for many seasons before the Hyas Tahmahnawis as he has directed our souls to follow.

I sense that the Hyas Tahmahnawis has chosen for me to understand that life is easily given and taken from us all upon our choosing to follow his path, or by accepting the path of the Meashchie Tahmahnawis, Bad Spirit.

Life is to be treasured as are the cool waters on a warm day.

Life is to be honored, as was the day when I sat upon the meadow's floor in silence, and as I sat and gazed around me I became one with all that surrounded me. Mowitch, deer, found shelter beside me, Kalakalas, birds, flew upon my shoulders, and kwiskwis, squirrels, played about my feet.

As I walk slowly amongst the forest many sticks I stop and peer deeply into the heart of a Cedar tree that I had visited beneath several times before. Upon its arms, striving to cling onto life itself, it offers refuge for new life to treasure upon its gathering host.

Thriving upon soften beds of green moss rises the beginnings of tomorrow's ferns. Small hairs rise up to meet Sun's warming rays as he crosses the heavens, and teardrops of the High Spirits that peer down upon us all each day find their pool within their bed's stream.

I was chosen to watch each form of life stirred by my entrance into their domains, and as I sat before them and silently watched them joined in play, I lent my ear to listen to all their voices, the deer and the elk as they fed in the meadow, to the pish as they plied the waters, and to the bees humming song, as well as the flutter of the butterflies wings. I sat and listened to the birds call across the river's course, and I listened to the voice of the wind as it passed benignly overhead.

As I sat beneath this Cedar that stretched far into the heavens all that I had seen and heard now journeyed to my side, and we were all as one within this kingdom, and to this Cedar.

We were alike brothers to the Earth . . .

Each of our own kind were chosen to our course in life, and to different ventures we were thrust towards our life's journey. But yet, we were all chosen to live upon our Illahee together, whether it be to just a day or to many.

Suddenly I realized the magnificence of this Cedar where I rested beneath, the Cedar too had reason and purpose to flourish amongst us all and reach higher to the very floor of the heavens that it reached out.

From its mother's seed first rose up her sapling, and from that sapling grew small buds upon its limbs, and from those limbs soon spread beautiful cones, and as the Cole breaths of winter chose its storm upon us, those same cones spilled softly to the soils beneath its rise and fed the squirrels so that they too would survive to see spring's wanting arrival.

Our gift this day was not just to one another, but to this single Cedar that arose from the soils of the earth and promised before every form of life, large or small, to its hosting pose before them.

As I peered towards Cedar's crown as it touched the crulean plain overhead, the heavens offered Cedar its repose below its softened cloud.

I gently ran my fingers across Cedar's trunk, and it was taken by my touch as it passionately swayed to the rhythm of the breeze, and as I too was swayed by its lasting dance beside me, Cedar lent to the lands sweet scent as it hung heavy upon the thick cushion of its bark and softly drifted down upon us.

My soul was taken completely by a beautiful light cast down by Otelagh as he passed overhead, and as it fell upon my face it pleasingly spread its warmth through Cedar's branch and quickly enveloped my soul.

As I sat below Cedar's sway and took of its sweet scent my eyes grew weary, and I was quick to fall fast asleep. As I slept I heard all the voices of the animals, of the pish, the snake and the lizard, the insects, as they all spoke of their passionate hearts as I dreamt alongside their gathering.

Many hours passed, and as I awoke Otelagh had fallen from the trail that he had taken and was now soon to fall below the Cascade's peak. It was then that I realized that it was only Great Cedar and myself that were swaying to our dance beneath the heaven of our kingdom.

Cedar and I were alone, and all the visitors that came to share their stories and of their plight given their surroundings were nowhere to be seen, and their concerns were brought heavily upon my shoulders as I sat beneath this cedar and asked, "why?"

I asked why there could not be peace between us all, and for all to share in the happiness that Otelagh's gift has offered?

As I was confused, I raised upon my knees and hailed unto the heavens and to the Hyas Tumtum for the answer so that my soul would find its rest once more.

As I knelt below Great Cedar's branching arms in wait for the Hyas Tumtum's answer, I was taken by a voice, though it was not sent from high above the heavens and above the clouds that solemnly passed overhead, but it was Great Cedar that now spoke.

Great Cedar's sway with the wind's rhythm now ceased, and I knew that what he had to share was to be of great importance.

Great Cedar asked, "What am I to these lands, and where do I to stand before the Hyas Tahmahnawis and amongst you all that pass upon my side?"

Great Cedar began to share of his birth many years ago from a tiny seed, and how that seed was watered by the winter's thaw that ran hurriedly across his root upon these grounds.

He shared that he has prospered upon these soils for many years and that he has witnessed many of his friends pass on their passion to their youth as they were then chosen to their soul's tour before their spirit's kingdom.

Great Cedar then questioned me if there was a mighty Cedar that was still chosen to rest upon the forest's floor behind us, and as I told him that there was only the root of that tree yet fastened to the ground from where it once proudly stood, Great Cedar's sorrow was deeply felt as he trembled beneath my lingering touch.

His voice too fell silent, and Great Cedar wavered unpromised to the wind's arising charm.

Great Cedar then sorrowfully shared that this was his mother that one day fell from upon her anchor to the soils many moons past as she grew old and weak. It was upon the most desperate of days Great Cedar shared that she clung tightly to his side and shared her love towards him for the final time.

He told me that as her arms slowly surrendered her tightened hold from his gathering branch her wail was then challenged unto all the trails of the heavens above, and her last breaths were shared of her praise to the Hyas Tumtum for all that he had awarded her.

Great Cedar told this was the last he would hear of her soothing song.

Again Great Cedar's sorrow was felt hardened within me, and as he wailed before the High Spirit's chairs, their tears fell hurriedly from upon their cheeks and washed away the pain from Great Cedar's soul.

I too knew of his sorrow as my mother was led to the heavens given her lonesome trail, and it was I that knelt upon her side as she gave praise before the Hyas Tumtum for all that she had treasured in her life, and as she passed with happiness attached to her lips and fell silent, her spirit was then fastened to the star chosen of her new home.

From high up behind the clouds that reigned heavily overhead, Otelagh again shined brightly upon Great Cedar's arms, and Great Cedar was soon pleased as he rose up from his flattened plain that he was grieved, and he praised Otelagh for his own soul's warming award.

I too was taken distant from my anguish and peered unto the heavens and smiled as Sun chose Great Cedar and I to share of one another's story.

Great Cedar and I stood tall beside one another for many hours that day at one another's sides as we shared of all that we had witnessed, and to all that our visions had shared upon us.

I told Great Cedar of walks that I had taken with my grandfather along this same beautiful river's fasten through our lands, and of my many visits beneath his own ascension as he grew strong and worthy before Otelagh's pass overhead each day.

I shared with Great Cedar that I was directed by his mother's sway to rest beneath his tower once I arrived beside their gathering.

I told him of the visions I had been taken, and to what lies just beyond the horizon's rising light that have yet to arrive.

I shared with Great Cedar of the battles fought between the Kloshe, Good, and the Mesahchie, Bad, Tahmahnawis for all our souls, and in these battles there would be many of our brothers lost from the ways of the good spirits, and that they would be led before the bad spirit's bludgeoned drum as he drew unto their lapse of faith and honor before our people's estimable trails.

I told him of the vision that I was chosen to witness as the skies would one day be cast in the same color as was our lost brothers blood if we were not to be promised of our march to the feet of the Mesahchie's telecasit and prey upon his lonely soul's appaling sway, and of our lead to our brother's return to the Hyas Tahmahnawis' directives and far from the Mesahchie Tahmahnawis' tightened grasp.

I told Great Cedar if we were not to take from the bad spirit's darkened purse to what was not his to take, the air that Great Cedar would then be forced to breath would be foul and distasteful, and given his disgust to our failure would then be thundered across the plains, through each of the kingdom's valleys, to the desert's tepid floor, across the seas from where our tribe first came, and to the highest of our spirit's peaks.

The air that he was to be forced to expel from his soul would then taint those that found their march through all the lands of our Earth, and all that the Hyas Otelagh had once treasured upon these lands we once knew would soon be lost, and not be seen again.

It was at that very stories end that Great Cedar shared that one day he had a vision as a small bird had chosen his welcoming branch and whispered softly to him that soon there would be many brothers from kingdom's that we had not heard that would discover the riches that our lands are awarded.

Great Cedar told that there would be peoples not held by our understanding to our ways as they would not only quickly take upon his soul, but of his sisters and brothers alike, as they would then cull all the forest's sticks to build their distant lodge.

He told me of the vision's promise that I would one day again journey to his side and rest beneath his cover before that day arrives, and if he were to share of this vision and of his passion to one day lie near his mother's bed that I would share of his worry to all those that would pass before my path, and that they would then pass on Great Cedar's vision, and his soul would then be saved to one day lie beside his mother.

I listened to Great Cedar and knew of his concern, and as I felt his worry hardened to his heart my head was bowed in shame before him. I too had shared that same vision and knew of these people's journey, and that as we were all connected by our own high spirits, we are all brought to bare as we inherently have allowed greed and our spiritless treks to be held in question from the very beginnings of our arrival upon this Earth.

We are known to customarily be seen quick to question to what shall we take from our visage upon Earth today, and be blind to all those tomorrows that are yet to rise upon our horizons.

I promised Great Cedar that I would stand guard over these lands as I had too promised our Hyas Spirits upon the Walls of Candor, and that no harm should befall his innocence below the trails that Otelagh crosses.

I promised Great Cedar that as we were brothers, and through his versed vision, we would not be taken by the spiritless soul of the Mesahchie Tahmahnawis that we all have troubled within us, but as I walk upon these treasured lands his vision shall be shared and heard by all those peoples that I should meet given of my journeys, and he too shall survive the error of our ways as shall our brother's promise to their return from the very entrance of the bad spirit's most darkened and unknowing tomb.

All life is to be honored and accepted so that it too can survive all that crosses before its path.

We all were permitted life by the gift of the Hyas Otelagh, Sun, and it is because of his hand that life depends to survive the play of the bad spirits as they too have reason to survive amongst us.

What is today has been for all the days that have passed, and what is to be seen of all the tomorrow is held within our hearts, as it is us that shall offer either life or death to the living souls that surround us.

It is our award by the High Spirit to justify through our acceptance of their life's definition, or we all shall one day be seen no more upon the bountied plains of our own kingdoms.

We must find ourselves seated before the Hyas Tahmahnawis' table and allow the breadth of his words to enter our hearts and souls, and we should not hear his speech with silenced thought and wander upon our Illahee without meaning and course.

Chapter 6
The Five Spirits

My father and I have shared many days exploring the lands and the waters that flow across them. The seasons were often shifting reigns beneath the skies above us as we shared their connection given our own beliefs to their presence amongst these lands.

I remember of our stay in this valley and of standing beneath the spirit's waters as the Sun grew warm above. It is these same waters that I call out for Loowit to extend her guidance to further allow me to my course of this trial with a positive understanding to my own rhthym amongst the spirited world that I am driven.

I have become weary as the Spirits have long disappeared as I last left the Hyas Stick and the Kokostick's song. I feel that the spirits that are bestowed upon these lands will not be proven of my worthiness before them.

It is the Great Eagle that I have not seen. It is the Great Eagle that must look down upon my path with respect and acceptance. Instead, I fear it has chosen to soar above lands distant to this and unwilling to cast his vote upon my cast to all the lands of our kingdom.

I have questioned the Spirit of Loowit's acceptance of my travels across these lands, and I ask, "What must I do?"

I question my readiness of this trek?

I question if I am to understand what I have seen as the truth.?

As I stand here, alone and confused to the avenues that hold the Spirit's trace, I question if I have misplaced my faith before their teachings and have accepted to my own lead?

I question if I have now crushed my father's soul before the Spirits have either accepted or denied my bid to honor my father's wish?

I have chosen to pass the silence of Loowit's charges and continue along the trail that is promised of my test before the spirits, though it was this same silence that my father told of that would deny my entrance beyond the Land's of the Lolo and into the kingdom of Wy-East.

My feet tread upon the rocky trail that travels into the realm of my own beginning to the change from dependence to independence, and then to examine the teachingss of my forefathers that will allow me to follow in their footsteps, as they too selected their traces across life's trails.

It is upon this very trail that I have chosen that allows me to begin to distinguish all that must be separated from my youth.

Upon my arrival before a tree's fallen spirit that lies across the mighty Eagle, I hear rising from the fast waters of the Evil Tumwata, Skoonichuk Falls, a message that has warned me of my passage beyond the ledge that I must cross.

"Nenamooks, if you dare to attempt to cross the mighty Eagle and enter our domain your soul shall be taken beneath the fast waters and never be seen again amongst the peoples of your village."

I know my quest must not stop at the request by the Evil Spirit's wishes, but I am drawn to the spirit's forewarning and have since yielded at the crossing of the Eagle below me.

As I stand at the foot of the cliff where thunderous roars can be heard rising from the Eagle's fast waters beneath me, and here my thoughts have become overwhelmed and I have allowed myself to hesitate toward my quest to search for the great Eagle's feather.

I experience fear in both my hesitation and by my wanting to continue, yet I know this very trial has been lain before many of our great forefathers, and they have all safely passed across the Eagle and scoffed at

Skoonichuk's baited breaths.

I tell myself that I must not waiver to my quest as does the Chinook's breeze across Great Sun's kingdom when the heat of summer is drawn to these lands.

As I stand across from the evil one and hear nothing that it speaks to my visage, I take upon my first step upon this fallen stick, and as I place my step, I too place faith in each and every step I take, and soon I have reached the far side of the Eagle.

My lesson here I understand is to not fear what is unseen, but to fear what lies within your soul that may stop your journey through life's opened arms. We must take away fear and initiate faith, and then we shall go far amongst the spirits that prosper upon the lands of our Illahee, Earth.

Towering to the skies, great boulders are held up to the heavens upon the edge of weathered walls. Below, the fallen spirits are covered with emerald tinted moss, unequaled in purity and proud against the surrounding water's fall.

Yielding my fate to this divine vision I hereby acknowledge to the Spirit of this ledge that I am worthy to stand amidst the gravity of its grotto.

Though the thunder of this Spirit's cascade roars within its tunneled walls and echoes once and twice again, I fear no evil as I enter within the darkness of this Great Spirit's den!

My understanding of this journey has permitted my entry into the Valley of the Eagle. My challenge now is determined within the darkness of this cave, whether my soul will pass through this gateway to the land's possessed by the Klale Lolo.

Will the world of spirits be as dark as their calling beneath this cascade?

I must remind myself that my travels are not manifested to the stars and that I must not pretend that my path is absolute.

To achieve greatness before my peoples I must be wise to defend them from the Mesahchie Tahmahnawis', Bad Spirits, that will be placed in defense before the Good Spirits, the Kloshe Tahmahnawis.

I must show my peoples the Mesahchie's contempt as we attempt our ascension before the Hyas Tumtum, the Great Spirit!"

I turn from this cavern's darkness and pursue the bend of this trail that I follow. Just as an eagle swiftly flies a flattened course across the boulders spewed out by the Great Wy-East, the Great Eagle's cry leads me to the tumwater so named the Eagle.

The very falls that my father had spoken of as we counseled before the blaze this past night.

With the swiftness of the Fox, the Hyas Opoots Talapus, and the veracity of the ravenous lolo the tumwater churns with seething anger as it dives and plunges to the darkened depths amidst the channel well hidden below.

I surrender my soul to the heavens in order that I may worship before the spirits of these lands. The wind has chosen its repose, and within the silence arises the cadence of the Spirit of the Eagle's chanting verse;

"My son! Though you have entered into our domain, you must be assertive. If you choose to be honored, you must be willing to cast your earthly ambitions before the water's of the Eagle. You must be absolute in your faithfullness towards the spirits of these majestic lands, and you must renounce the ways of your mortal delusions before your peoples in order that you can be sanctioned within the kingdom of the Saghalie Tyee. It is certain that they must be commanding of their strength, for a journey such as they are to encounter and in their journey many will find fear, and in this unfaithfulness, they may easily cast their souls silent and become devoured by the Mesahchie Tahmahnawis of the Klale Lolo."

My coming before this stream's currents is unerring as my father once spoke of our tribe's gathering within this magnificent stadium that lies some distance beyond the borders of its hold.

He spoke of many gatherings of our peoples upon these grounds as they prepared to thank the Hyas Spirits for the gift of food and shelter.

It is before these same spirits that our peoples perform a dance for many turns of the moon and chant for the sun's returning warmth.

As many tribes of our nation journeyed to this canyon to offer their respect before the spirits, here we have joined as brothers and have feasted upon the gifts of Metlako and fed heartily on the moolack's souls.

Chapter 7
The Trail of Principles

As Sun has journeyed far from our heavens above us, I have approached the shores of our river and as I stand peering across our its rush I see my village.

The rising smoke of our camp's fires along the shore can be seen from the opposite horizons as they swirl skyward into the eastern winds.

Upon the bank of the Great River I know where my father is now reflecting at this hour. It is there where I can remember him sitting along the river's brace where we have shared so many memories of the journeys that he has undertaken and of those we have shared.

I sense my father longed that my lessons would one day allow me to lead our peoples safely upon these lands. My awareness of my father's wishes has taught me also the wisdom of my father's plea before the Spirits to allow my vision to extend beyond the lessons of those less fortunate.

By my father's guidance, I shall not be judged as the destroyer of his dreams!

Nor will I be discovered unbridled towards my own!

As I have journeyed to these lands many times with my father I know that the remainder of the tumwaters are tethered to the cliffs that rise far above the valley, and are found upon the grounds held sovereign by Multnomah.

My father had always forbid me to enter the Lands of Wah until my life had begun to seperate from my youthful ways, and with outstretched arms, I must first plead to the High Spirits as I grasped tightly to the maturity of a young brave.

My presence before the Spirits of these tumwaters had to await their blessing.

When I was unfledged, I did not understand his wishes to restrain me from approaching these waters.

I have now traveled boldly through the morning and into the latter hours of this day, and as I approach the stream's embrace I have notably marked numerous salmon as they are tightly gathered beside the boulders that are held within its shadow.

I find the salmon committed to their challenge of one another as they seek calm waters that are hidden from the stream's gathering fury.

Our people, belonging to the Chinook Nation, and the nations that adhere to the lands of Pahto, as they are of the great Yakima and Klickitat, gather upon these Hyas grounds as the leaves return to the arms of the trees and new life begins to emerge from the shadow's of the forest.

We name this gathering, the Illahee Hiyu Muckamuck, Earth Festival.

As I witness to the wind's compelling voice along the walls of the cliff upon my entrance to the valley of Wahclella, the Spirits have begun to speak

"As we have graciously permitted Munra's honorable placement before you, your approach to the Legend's of Wahclella is protected by her foreboding and ever potent guard.

Her sincere demeanor will judge all who boldly pass before her. If you find yourself accepting of Munra's honor, Munra shall permit your passage alongside the hallowed walls of Wahclella, and unto the sacred walls of Wahclella, cast your mortal illusions from your soul and take up the passions that the Council so demands."

My thoughts ponder the unthinkable once again, and I find myself hesitant as I do not understand fully their request or of their demands!

As I stand before you, "I ask of you, the Great Spirit of Munra, to accept my worthiness and be assured of my mettle.

I accept all the Hyas Spirits belonging to Wahclella, and the respected entrance of these sacred lands, where all those that enter must be challenged to their vision."

As I stand in wait for Munra's judgment an icy chill clings taut to my soul!

"I, Munra, the guardian before the gates beholding to the spirits and theCouncil of Wahclella have been cautioned by the Council of the Great Chinook.

You must realize my sternest caution towards any unceremonious disputes and treachery towards Wahclella's hallowed grounds and sanctified waters.

Profess before me that you understand my guarded words and of my duty to the Council of Wahclella!

Be absolved of all your earthly thoughts and be well visioned to the spirits that shall appear before you. For they are the spirits that shall approve or deny your passage throughout the lands owned by the Eagle and of Wah!"

As the trail has once again descended from the heights that I had traveled, I find the roar of this canyon unmistakably created by the water's dive into the darkened pool within its circular cask.

I am amazed as I stand fronting the water's descention into Wahclella's widened bowl as the water's fall happily within its opened hands.

As I stand stunned by the beauty of this Falls I am overwhelmed, and as my mind is anchored by the tumwater's roar, I can scarcely discern the voices that resonate from upon Wahclella's cliff that are demanding of my attention.

As I unconsciously hesitate to answer their calling from above I am quickly repentant of my delay before the legend's most distinguished appearance as they honorably speak before me!

Upon the mercy of the Council I dared myself to speak; "I am yet a servant and have appeared before you to accept your teachings. I plead for your understanding in that I have not lain witness to such a remarked hall as you have gathered before me.

"Accept my eagerness to witness unto your Holy Stage as these grounds shall be my witness unto your greatness!

"I fear not the decisions that you establish as I stand before you as a child accepting of your keep, permit me to hear your judgment.

"I shall gather my peoples and plead for the honor that it brings us as you accept our presence upon your lands, and of your unselfish and gratuitous offerings that shall safely lead our peoples from the Mesahchie Tahmahnawis!

I stand before the Council's review and observe Sun passing overhead. It seems to be unquestionably obedient to the moon's definitive and cloaking change!

I fear that the similarity between the day's beginning and ending may be subject for my dismissal by the spirits as they linger.

I am appalled by my perception that my soul is to be thrown to the canyon floor from the heights of Wahclella's crown if I am not allowed to attend the teachings of the Council of Wahclella. I bend my thoughts toward acceptance or my quest may quickly become dissolved.

From above the walls holding this canyon as they command the water's graceful fall arise the spirits' invincible and resounding voices once more.

The resonation of their words upon these grounds beneath me repeat and demand my prompt attention!

I find their poignant speech terse . . .

Nenamooks!

"Whispering through the trees you may detect the voices of long past legends as we chant of the magical lands that stand before you.

Consumed upon the foundation of these lands with emerald ferns and magnificent stands of cedar, we, the council of these hallowed grounds, deem this land forever sacred, as the benevolence of life bequeathed amidst the cascades of these descending waters sincerely deliver substance unto your mere creation.

Towering far into the heavens stand proudly the pillars of candor as they are firmly planted and a true witness against man's deceptive truths.

For we, the Council of Wahclella, shall not permit treachery nor dishonesty!

Nature's glory stands before all man, and its gift must not be ravaged by man's selfish or ignorant ambitions.

For you Nenamooks, given your acceptance of our chanting wail shall then be determined to uphold and defend these hallowed grounds of its rightful honor.

Hallowed are these walls that your spirits are treasured!

Hallowed are these waters that permit the cleansing of your soul!

To those whom are commissioned before our counsel, may it be established just!

As we, the Council upholding to Wahclella are continually found auspicious and absolute upon these eternal and sequential truths . . . .

I had first thought that the beauty of this canyon and the life that flourishes upon its grounds were the essential matters to become treasured within my soul. I find myself yearning the legends of our tribes as they have permitted our peoples to have faith in their lead, and to gain hope for better tomorrows beneath their reign, and to dream of one day where life is connected by all and all is promised to their safe keep amongst one another.

I must be gathered to the Spirit's likenesses and promote our treasured lands before all those whom pass upon them!

To the furthest borders of these lands I shall extend my travels, and I shall not waver upon a corner of their share.

The teachings of our *Hyas Tahmahnawis* must be respected by our peoples against the day they may grumble and doubt toward our placement upon these treasured and enamored lands once the days turn dark, and we find ourselves wandering from their tightened grasp to our wayward souls!

"*Hyas Tahmahnawis!*

I promise to uphold your presence before my peoples so that they may be deserving to stand before you.

If you approve my quest and of my commission before all peoples that I pass upon my journeys, I shall plead for your guidance that your principles shall be known and extended to all peoples upon our coupled path."

As I have spoken my soul to the Council of *Wahclella* I envisioned a *Kulakula's* soar upon the thermals. It passes before me and enters the spaciousness of the clouds and I see that it is the celebrated *Pil Opoots ChakChak*, Red Tail Hawk.

My peoples have learned of our *ChakChak's* tumultuous ways and have held its presence safely within our hearts for many suns.

Our ceremonial dances before our Spirits have told tales of the Great *ChakChak's* traits, and we have felt the *ChakChak's* presence at our sanctioning upon these glorious grounds, a gift acquired from the *Hyas Tahmahnawis'* shield as he overlooks us all upon the trails that we each search out for our direction in life beneath his leading hand.

As the *ChakChak* departs far into the western skies, I hasten my steps to follow his flight!

Chapter 8
Elowah's Survival

I have been guided by the visions of the Hyas Spirits as I have walked through the forest that lines the great river below me in silence, and as I enter the canyon where lies the grounds of Elowah, I am captured by her towering form far above me as she holds strong to the clouds claimed by the heavens.

Long ago it was told that Elowah chose before those that were pointed along their course of their quest to have explained of her honorable stature above the Lands of Wah.

I remember well the words that my grandfather once spoke of her strength and will to survive all the winter's storms that razed across her fractured face as she shared before him;

"I, the Spirit enlisted to this canyon have acquired from the Hyas Spirit of Wah the understanding that mankind must resist temptation to all the Mesachie Tahmahnawis' that dwell amongst us as land and life must not fall victim upon their whetted soils, but must flourish amongst all properties that embrace the entirety of our brother's nations upon earth if we too are to survive."

I ponder Elowah's majestic face. Sun has adorned her grounds with a variety of flowers in all that surrounds her waters.

Amongst the fragments fallen from Elowah's fractured face I find the malicious winter's tempest has scoured Elowah's face with their attacks as had my father once told.

Elowah speaks, "As I have been fastened throughout the centuries upon the high ledges, I have witnessed the transformations of your peoples upon these imposing lands.

"When your peoples' stand beneath my rise I have been attentive to their questions and have known of their admiration of my imperialistic waters as they fall before them.

"I have heard the tales that have followed my ascension before the throne of Hyas Metlako, and I have stood proudly before the stories that your people have stirred within my soul.

"Yes, I have a question that has lingered throughout the many suns and moons that have passed overhead for the ears of a great man that I was told one day would appear before me. A man that was soon to become the Chief to the peoples upon the Land's of Wah that would only take from these lands of our kingdom to what his peoples must use to sustain their preservation within its borders. A leader amongst all peoples that would foresee the rise of what is good and what is bad within them, and that he too would become marked to each of our spirit's understandings and speak of only the truths that we each share before him.

"I know as you have chosen the trails that have taught you the significance of our existence that you may soon command your peoples and place on them the duty of supporting all life that tread upon these sacred grounds.

"One day as Sun begins to pass beyond the heaven's trail, and the moon aspires to the shadow's lengthened stretch upon our grounds, your peoples shall all be gathered before the Hyas Tumtum. Your peoples shall then dance before the High Spirit and cast off their longing that had once condemned them before the table of the Bad Spirits.

"Your peoples, the followers of our ways, shall then be seen placed upon the stage of these glorious lands and your efforts shall then be continually seen throughout the passing moons and the rise of all the following suns.

"Your guidance shall become cause to your people's rise before the Hyas Tahmahnawis' most honored seat!

"My question to you, as you stand before me Nenamooks, if I, Elowah, the Spirit that penetrates the souls of all those that pass fronting my presence am asked of my pledge toward your seat before all our peoples, what may you offer the Spirits and to those peoples who will pass amongst the treasured lands that we now inhabit?

"My acceptance of your placement upon this chair must be met by my estimation of your honor and of your integrity toward all the lessons and gifts that you have been chosen to interpret.

"I ask you only to speak the truth of your heart and of your soul. By these stated truths you hereby promise shall be marked upon these lands and before the Hyas Tahmahnawis, and only then shall you become the founding brother of all the life forms placed upon the soils of our earth by the Great Spirit.

"Upon my acceptance as I sit before the table of your Hyas Spirits, you and all your circle shall sit honorably before the formidable and magnificent Chinook Nation."

As Elowah completed her words, my mind has been cleansed from what was once my selfish desires that remained of my youthful ways, and her words has chosen my vision to my quest in life to accept a different and more aspiring path to challenge myself.

I stand unafraid before Elowah's presence for Elowah's most profound query has set me upon a path that I had not suspected throughout the days of my youth.

The philosophy of the Spirits has allowed me to glimpse into their souls, as they too have found their course across these lands and have had to stand forthright before Elowah's challenge.

To know the truth and speak it clearly!

I remember that as my peoples were gathered before the fires of our council my father spoke the truth. There were many braves of our camp that had undertaken the rites before the Lands of Wah, and I recall that not one had spoken of Elowah's challenge.

My mind has seen the darken clouds of storm's past hold strong within it as I was once confused of my draw to these land's most spiritual revelations. But as I find the magnitude of my rite before Elowah's charges, they have swept away the question of my worth and direction across these lands as well they were swept distant before my brothers, as Elowah's spirit has led me to the Hyas Tahmahnawis' creation as I resolve to allow all life to live and prosper upon this, our only Illahee.

My weakness, as I understand, is bound by my mortality upon this earth.

I know once I approach the end of my life the Hyas Spirits must be assured that their ways are accepted and honored if I were to join them upon Wahclella's binding truss.

I can envision the lands of the rising sun to the east, and I can perceive the sands beneath my feet as the great sun chooses to slip beyond the trails of the heavens to the west.

I can envision the great mountains that our peoples have been known to climb, and I can visualize a landscape to the south where the fierceness of the Fire Spirit that lives within the great Lassen, and I look upon the frozen ice fields of the north that once held the influence of Missoula behind their dam.

In all these visions, all the kingdoms must survive today as they have survived all the days before, and as our peoples walk the many trails that lead to and from these kingdoms, they too shall be survived by their young if we all find respect and offer our hearts and souls to their rightful accommodation before us.

I, Nenamooks, shall one day share my possessions as they were shared by the Great Spirits of these extraordinary Lands of Wah.

Our misunderstandings must not turn us away from the Spirits of our Illahee. For one day we shall pass through all the tomorrows, across all the suns and moons, into where eternity holds no border.

My answer before Elowah is held in the teachings of my father and all the Spirits who have come to rule upon our lands;

Is I stand beneath Elowah my answer rises to the very crown of her tower, "Elowah, as I enter within the gateways that our chief's had once stepped, I shall proclaim to all our brothers the words that our Hyas Illahee has manifest to our survival.

In our visions we must see beyond the rising sun of today and witness the disease and waste our brothers shall one day spread across all the lands as Sun sets upon our own creation. Our misuse of these properties shall bring shame before the Great Spirit and shall allow the Hyas Tahmahnawis to mistrust our judgment. Through our forefather's visions we will have forced the extinction of many gifts that were chosen to live amongst us all, and had been offered before us upon this Earth.

I, Nenamooks, shall take upon my soul to walk amongst the trails of all our spirits so that our peoples shall devote their lives in demanding respect for all that is natural that you have most honorably placed before us, as all that is is brought forth to us is through your own creation!"

Upon the completion of my answer to Elowah's question, the great winds of the Chinook coursed the trails of the mountains and of the plains, and swept beyond the bordered channels of our waters and across the great waters where Sun now sleeps, and all was then again discovered privilaged beneath Otelagh's fastened race across the heavens . . .

Chapter 9
The Skookum Spirits Within Us

I have chosen to follow the righteous path where the Spirits have led me and have allowed my soul to settle in the peacefulness of their wisdom. As these lessons are dispersed to all the tribes of our peoples they shall profit by the Hyas Tahmahnawis' philosophy.

Not only shall we profit before the eyes of the Great Spirits, but we shall also become one with all mankind and inhabit forever the lands alongside the animals and plants that bring life upon the soils of our Great Illahee.

I must rest my weary legs as my journey is soon destined toward the Hyas Tahmahnawis of the Great Multnomah.

When I approach this canyon's impressive wall I see the Tahmahnawis' challenge as he assuredly soars above my diminutive cast upon these grounds.

As I silently progress through the sticks of our forest, my thoughts are altered by an impressive gathering of deer and elk that lie before me.

As I am breathless at their numbers, I find myself honored to sit and share their gathering as my presence is well hidden from their sights!

There is meaning to their numbers, yet I find no answer from my father's past teachings that shares their cause, as it is not the winter's harassing storm that draws their numbers into the lowland's flattened floor.

The wind stirs amongst the early evening's shadow. I see the herd's leisure before me, and I can hear the solitary call of a coyote's soul. Her call runs upon the trails and confirms that she moves cautiously through the hidden hollows of the Valley of the Eagle and into these Lands of Wah.

Our peoples have held firmly to the legend of the coyote, and her repetitive howling enlists the shadows of the night as she intently searches for her illustrious and truant mate.

The tale of the Talupus contends that she fears her mate to have been cast to the spirits above upon the frozen fields secured by the ice and snow glistened upon the great peaks of the Cascades.

Her cries are lost into the early evening shadows, and she executes her swift departure condemning all that live within the Lands of Wah as she searches.

Her grievance is directed upward toward the noble and sanctioned moon as I have seen her standing upon the highest mountain's top as Moon rises from behind the shadows of Wy-East.

Her howl confirms to her desperation as she continually howls to the distant and fading stars.

She never settles upon the mountains that she climbs, nor does she lapse beneath the waters as she reports upon her grievious loss.

Given to our peoples throughout The Valley of the Eagle and the Magical Land's of Wah she perpetually searches for her truant mate.

Long into the darkened hours I have discovered within my soul the compassion to accept her unforgiving dirge.

As the legends of the Talupus have been shared throughout by the teachings of the elders of my tribe, the Talupus' eagerness to once again discover her mate has brought Princess Lawala Clough to beckon the Great Spirits of Wy-East and Pahto to extend their mighty powers and exalt the Talupus as a legend before these lands.

The Spirits that have taken the Talupus' mate are known to appear only amongst the shadows that spread across the lands. As the day's warming light secedes to the cold and bitter darkness it causes the Mesahchie Tahmahnawis to rise up in their misty habitation and take from us those souls that wander far from where their spirit once held strong.

These same Spirits cage the good skookums of the forests while the Mesahchie Skookums begin their perverse and daunted haunt for our souls. Mankind's maladies are brought to bear as the Mesahchie Skookums allow the confluence of righteousness and strife to darken our hearts making us appear disgraceful before the Hyas Spirits.

As I sit and contemplate the presence of these Spirits in our lives, I believe the path that leads me past their black words may also grant the requisition of the feather belonging to the Eagle!

I must be understanding of not only what reverence lies within my peoples, but I must also be aware of the evil that stirs our mortal souls.

I must attack these evil Skookum Spirits.

I must teach my brothers of the good that they have inherited from our ancestors, and explain the consequences of these Skookum Spirit's poach amongst our gathering upon these lands.

I must petition before the Hyas Tahmahnawis for my brother's souls to be spared the evilness of the Skookum Spirits!

If my brothers forsake our compassionate ways, if they choose to wander far from our beliefs of the High Spirit, they must be accepting and aware that punishment before the Hyas Tahmahnawis' table is to be banned from our nation, the Great Chinook.

Our lost brothers shall be banished to the lands of the lolo, and burned by the fire spewed from within Wy-East's fuming and searing depths.

I sense that many of our family shall shy away from their misdeeds as they envision their fate.

Yet I grieve that there are many that shall run the trail of the Talupus and be lost to us forever.

As I sit quietly before these moolack and mowitch the gathering of their herd reminds me of mankind as we are gathered amongst our own huddled and restless masses.

Although I may one day be exhalted before my peoples, I must also understand that my resolve before them is not created by my own cause, but in what I have learned and have accepted through the Great Spirit's teachings.

I must be certain to attend to both the good and to the evil of our kind!

I must be as selfless to both, the good and the evil, as all members of our family must be given the opportunity to flourish.

We must attend the revelations that our Spirit's share.

As my eyes open I am awakened by the kalakala's screams above me as I find myself lain against a tree as Sun begins to rise above the distant horizon.

As I search the forest and the great meadow beneath I discover that the moolack and mowitch have journeyed distant to where they last stood below me. As I walk amongst the openness of the field I find no evidence that their hoofs have stepped soundly upon this grassy meadow.

I ask, what have I seen if it were not the moolack and mowitch? Yet, I have the memory of their words spelled deeply within my soul to share!

My step has quickend, I am allowed only five days to conclude my lessons before the Hyas Spirits. I must stand bravely before my peoples. If my brothers delay their approval, I must then accept the expulsion as it may be granted by the Spirits, and I shall be lost upon the land's of the lolo until my return has been again granted by the Spirits.

My shame shall then be assured!

Chapter 10
The Healing Waters of Oneonta

This morning I stand before a plunging tumwater that resembles the tail of a horse kuitan opoots, as it falls from the high cliff.

The cliffs that rise above this valley and the Hyas Columbia have been shaped throughout the centuries by Wy-East and the jealousy of the Hyas Missoula.

I have been told by my father that this is where the keepers of the Spirit's herds lead the kuitans and allow their ceaseless play. I have been told the ponies that are given to the herd are held safely higher on this hillside as they too are allowed their muse within another tumwater.

My father shared that these waters were first formed from three plumes of the great heron that rests high above their gathering herd.

Upon my arrival before Oneonta's Gorge I have noticed

Sun has not yet risen above the forest's sticks and has not shed its warmth upon the creek bank's soils as the walls of this canyon's cave allows it to be well concealed.

I am hesitant to challenge this waterfall's hide as I stand before its gate, hearing its call I must obey its command and accept whatever my fate is to be, or fail in my attempt to capture the feather of the Eagle that I have come to yearn.

As I approach the enclosure of Oneonta's Gorge's formidable doors I have again found myself easily challenged as the fallen souls of the *forest lies besieged and withdrawn from their rise unto the heavens by the Skookum Tahmahnawis as winter's storms have wrought their fallen souls to lie piled and lifeless upon its darkened entrance.*

I am saddened as I cross over the trees that now lie stilled and silent to the rythym of the earth. Upon every step I climb upon them I mourn for their loss amongst their brothers and sisters and hope to hear of their pleading voice

Yet, they say nothing . . .

As I find myself emerged within the water's rush I have been led along her towering walls and below the falls where Oneonta's call can be heard to follow the flow of her waters.

My son! You have conquered the challenges that I have set before you. So now I have chosen to share with you my teachings as they have been drawn from the birth of this kingdom.

"As I choose to speak before you I shall be asking for your review beside my pious walls and ask of you to become impassioned to the words that I share before you, and that you grasp the truths of my words that shall allow you the wisdom that I have assembled within my clutch.

As I sit and heed the lesson of Oneonta I can hear the lowly chants of many chiefs that have once led our peoples through our supporting reign upon these lands that we owe our lives.

The waters that are cast before my feet are engrossed with teachings that focus on the harmony of the life forms we know within our kingdom.

I find these waters are pure as all life that abounds upon the soils of the earth shall find their challenge from another's condemning attacks quickly gained by the vision that Oneonta shares to the compassionate thoughts that we must share before all their visage.

As I stand before her chair high above me Oneonta speaks of the magic that this water holds within its course to the great river below. She explains that the Great Salmon that arrive home brings with them new life as they offer their souls to mold with the lands that they pass, and new life shall arise from the soils each season.

The Spirit of Oneonta has spoken well as her words pierce deep within me and through the tautness of my mortal soul I understand.

I believe that in all life, from the harassing fly, to the stinging bee, and of the softened petals of the flowers, that all lend their likenesses to the survival of all the species that thrive upon the soil and in the waters of our Great Earth.

The Spirit of Oneonta has requested that mankind must insure that the fauna and creatures alike are promised their keep upon these lands as they have persisted from the days before our own beginnings.

Our measure as guardians of these emerald lands must be guarded by discovering the harmony between all that lives, and in our willingness to save the minuteness of its being.

I believe that the Spirits promised to Wahclella must be related to Oneonta, as they have both ferverently chosen to preserve the Valley of the Eagle and the Lands of Wah, and to all the properties witnessing of their modeled kingdoms.

The significance of our hold on Earth's treasures must be found unchallenged yet we must manifest all that the Spirit's decree.

It is profound that we are continually invited to partake of our Illahee's promise even though one day Sun will not pass overhead, and there shall be no sustenance to extend our own survival!

I shall willingly pledge before the Spirits that mankind shall be timelessly welcomed upon these trails, and through our laborious efforts these lands shall remain as innocent as the day of their extraordinary birth.

Or upon a dark and shrouded day our failure shall insuringly allow mankind to become the victors of our own definitived defeat!

We must believe that the Spirits solemnly grasp the answers that shall permit all life to prosper.

We must allow life, either large or small to be given its rightful stature beside us, and to flourish as they insure our own survival!

Chapter 11
Isick Opoots

I understand that the stages the Hyas Tahmahnawis has set before me must now be distinguished in my own thoughts, and their delegation that must be placed before mankind in order that all life may survive.

I have found myself longing for the Spirit's support as I attempt to follow the pathways of my trial as I stand before the swift current of this river. It appears hostile to my survival if I were to attempt its cross. As I stood questioning my efforts a great beaver has swam before me.

This beaver I shall name Isick Opoots, Paddle Tail.

Isick has told me if I were to allow him to speak of the importance that his family attached to the waters that flowed from the winter snows upon the Spirit's most heralding peaks that he would guide me to the distant shore and allow my passage safely across its frothing form.

I silently question his request and have accepted myself to be at his mercy, and have since agreed to his wish.

He begun to speak of the meadows that his families created as they dammed the water's rush to the great river beneath the Cascade's hold.

I found Isick to be a wise male, and to my amazement he swam effortlessly through the swift currents of this river.

"My family have been honored within the streams of these lands by the Spirits, and our families have also been sacrificed by the misdeeds as your people have unjustly taken our spirit in order that you may be found warming your souls from the winter's frozen breaths."

As Isick spoke of his family's demise within these meadows, I found myself sharing his sorrows as he named his brothers and sisters that were sadly taken from their watery Illahee.

He continued to share many stories that he had encountered as the trees surrounding his home grew new leaves, and that they were seen plentiful upon the outstretched arms of their welcoming host. He spoke of how the waters drew within the meadow's plane and created a haven for the duck and goose, and that it held as its gift, freedom for all creatures to co-exist.

Isick shared many a summer's passing, and said before the time his family had arrived upon these lands that there were many stories told of the mighty waters that were created by the frozen breaths exhaled from the Great Missioula, and that Missioula's waters were sent to flood the lowlands that stand submerged beside the Great Columbia.

He also expressed his grief toward the droughts that had lain open many wounds to the animals that had once formed their alliance upon the grounds that we now shared.

I stood listening to his every breath and I saw Isick become quite sullen as he recalled the story of a brood of geese that had wandered aimlessly in search for water to find food and shelter within its watery depths for their young.

These geese were tortured by the heated soils of the dry and barren lands that they had scoured. As they searched for water, a red fox had stalked them and suddenly charged, and quickly devoured the young of their brood before they could defend against the kahkwa pil talupus' charge.

I sensed that he may have indeed seen the fox gorge upon their chick's souls, yet he spoke as if the story had been passed down by the animals of his kingdom.

Isick stated that as the geese were pleading for the water's return, Isick's family was petitioned to challenge the water's escape to the mighty Columbia by Oterlagh as he passed overhead one day.

Isick and his family were chosen to build the dams that would hold the waters within the boundaries of the forest's cover before they insisted upon their fall to the Great Columbia. The meadows, he stated, would then again teem with new life, and the animals would return to their watery homes and find shelter and safety beneath the new life that would quickly emerge from the soils.

Isick also knew that the marsh would always emerge unharmed from the winter's freeze. The spring thaw would bring the return of all the creatures, and of all the plants of the forests, and of the meadows.

Isick stated; "The creatures of these lands should be allowed to breath life into the next generation. We trust the Spirits of the Sticks. Our families shall live and prosper upon these lands, and we shall survive until the warm light of Sun dims to darkness' daunting and eternal chill.

These words were the last that Isick had chosen for me to hear as he then swam silently along the river's course and led me safely across his lodge as it was firmly embedded across the meadow's extended floor.

Isick's spirit shall linger forever in my teachings. I promise before the Great Eena Spirit that I shall not allow my people's traps to be lain near his people's village, so that Isick's family's souls will not warm our shoulders as winter's spirit breaths harshly upon us and falls heavily upon our village, and to these lands.

Chapter 12
The Great Missoula

My retreat down this slope has stirred my memories of the Great Falls that I had seen as my father and I had visited our brothers, the Multnomah, at a village downstream along the great river. Our journey to the Multnomah was taken during the years of my youth, and yes, I can still envision the water's thunderous rumble from the cliff's reach beneath the clouds.

I know I am soon to appear again before its majestic form, and that I may be challenged by the Great Spirits that it must share.

My father had grown to admire the chief of the Multnomahs' for his leadership.

The Multnomahs' were well respected by all the tribes of our nation as they waded amongst the marshes and caught the hahthaht, duck, and kalakalama, goose, that arrive with the fall of the stick's golden and crimson leaves from upon their outstretched arms.

We have traded with the peoples of Multnomah and with the village of Cathlapotle that lies further along the river's course to the Great Waters.

We have been fortunate to have traded for our brother's goods as they have allowed our peoples to survive the harrassing winter's storms that have left our peoples unable to stalk and lure the souls of the moolack and mowitch upon their frozen grounds.

Since I had visited their kindred fires with my father Sun has passed across the heavens of our skies many times, and yet I recall one night as my father and I sat before the fires of the Multnomah's village, and it was that night that we were told the story of the Great River and of all the lands that once were lain beneath its fastened wake.

Their story began as our Hyas Spirits first came upon the lands of Wah and were first formed by Wy-East, Pahto, and Lawala Clough. The heated bursts from these Spirits had ceased, and the

Cascades were then recreated by the Spirit of Missoula as he ruled the kingdoms of the frozen north and released his temper towards the southern borders of his reign.

The Great Missoula's Spirit was angered by the ways of the peoples that inhabited the banks of his treasured kingdoms to the south, and as punishment to all those that lived beside his waters he gathered great mountains of rocks and ice as Otelagh passed over him and shared no warmth to his soul for many moons, and the waters then collected mightly behind the silence of his dam.

With the thrust of Missoula's mighty spear the frozen waters began to burst from behind their harried banks and swiftly coursed through the river's distant valleys, The waters quickly spread to the south and west as they were frenzied for their escape into the waters of the great salt chuck.

The emergence of these waters as they coursed high above the lowlands floors were punishing to the banks of the Columbia and upon Wy-East's lands. Upon their arrival to our kingdom the Spirit of Wy-East was quickly found spewing his distrust and anger at the Great Missoula and of his wanting breach.

As Missoula's waters were found scouring the canyon's walls completely, Wy-East was greatly saddened as he had first created the canyons and allowed the river's forms to be pronounced by his own hand.

It was then that Wy-East chose his bed to lie high above the Valley of the Eagle and to The Lands of Wah and allowed the rise of the Cascades beside him, and once the floods of Missoula crossed over Wy-East's lands for the last day, Wy-East again chose to craft his most inventive and impressived forms upon Missoula's wasteful attack.

The tumwaters from which our peoples measure their significance upon these lands was Wy-East's gift as he shared his enthusiasm and artistry upon the mighty Missioula's wayward throes.

This tale has been shared throughout the years from the birth of the Valley of the Eagle and of the Land's of Wah, and it is treasured today as the origin of Great Missoula's envy towards the Great Wy-East, and of Wy-East's lands as they are now gloriously spread enrichened with life by the soils thrust from beneath his sanctioned grounds.

The challenges that the Spirits of these tumwaters have confronted have truly given these fertile lands honor amongst all the heavenly bodies that are treasured before the land's of this Earth.

To those peoples granted the courage of Elowah to honor the Earth as they do the heavens above as she too has withstood all charges upon these lands, to those peoples that savor the wisdom spoken by the Council of Wahclella, to them is given honor before all the peoples of the Earth for all the days that Sun is to pass overhead.

Their existence shall be welcomed upon their spirit's own passing as they shall arrive before the gates of the Hyas Tumtum's Village with opened arms.

Chapter 13
The Great Chak Chak

I have selectively retraced the very steps that my ancestors have taken, and as I acquire the harmony that these Lands of Wah hold within me I have been taken before the judgment of a Fish Eagle as I observe its soar above the water.

Nearing the form of the Great Multnomah I have scanned the tree line along the shores of our esteemed river, and I hear within the whispering breaths of the Chinook the cries of the young of a Fish Eagle as they sit upon the branching arms of their stick's lodge.

I recall one afternoon as my father and I traveled through these majestic lands as we stood admiring the fall of Multnomah a great shadow was cast above us as a ChakChak had quickly maneuvered its flight from the water's surface and rose beyond the stick's foremost heights.

My father and I were both amazed at the simplicity of the ChakChak's breathless flight above us as it surrendered its gracefulness to the winds above Multnomah's cliff and perched upon the limb of a tree.

The majesticness of the fish eagle has been admired by our peoples for all the suns that have passed overhead, and I recall the tale of a Great Visionary that had entered our village and spoke to our brothers as he defined the importance that the Hyas ChakChak signified to all life that relinquish their souls to the Kloshe Tahmahnawis of these lands.

The story began one day as this distant brother of all the peoples of all the lands that we are not known, a speaker and visionary to and for the animals of this Illahee alike entered into our encampment. He stood before our peoples as he professed that if we were not promised to all the land's preservation that we would be found disgraced before the Hyas Spirits as they would disassociate the ChakChak's team from our own, and the ChakChaks would then disappear and attach themselves above another tribe.

As this prophetic traveler continued to educate our peoples he stated that he feared that mankind's selfishness towards the life forms that are found sacred to our nations shall bring forth our distraction by the same Spirits that hold our lives in safety.

He has shared the magnificence of the ChakChak, and how its Spirit has allowed our families to pass freely beneath their breathless and examining flights.

He stated, "You shall find our Great ChakChak, the Great Fish Eagle Spirit, shrieking unto the winds as she flies beyond the sullen shores of our troubled waters. By her flight into the heavens and beyond our reach, one day we shall learn to fear her angry cries.

"Upon freedom's wings our Great Spirit shall tend collectively to her expeditious flight, and she shall be seen earnestly soaring into the heavens to flee our injustices as they have been placed upon the lands.

"If we fail to convince our Great Fish Eagle of our honor to her perceptions, we shall certainly discover the Eagle gloomly peering exhaustively upon the sores erupting upon her once treasured and hallowed shores.

"My children, I must contend that the mighty Eagle Spirit that lingers upon the breadths of the heavens must look positively down upon this Earth and accept the environment that we share.

"I have seen within my visions the mighty buffalo of the plains as they were once known to number as great as the sticks of our forests. In my vision I have seen them fade from the rolling plains of the rising sun.

"By this same vision, we must not allow the Mesahchie Spirits to steal what lies heavily upon our hearts.

"We must be as teachers and bring all mankind to understand the wisdom of allowing life to safely flourish amongst us.

"We must show to all our brothers that life as they see it today shall be sternly judged, and they shall be awarded for their treachery by the Mesahchie Tahmahnawis' most grievous shadow.

As the Great Spirits find those peoples linked to the sanctity of the soils of the kingdoms that they honor, so

Shall they too be honored.

"If all mankind are to be found incompetent, the Earth shall be burned by the heat that the Great Spirits command within their unyielding powers!

"I have seen, given my visions by the Great Spirits, that if earth is to survive, we must be sincerely taken by the honor that we are granted by the Kloshe Tahmahnawis as we live and propagate amongst the life forms that we pass, and we must allow each species to flourish as they were first born to this Earth.

"Mankind was chosen to the soil's of this Earth as were the Great Spirits before us, and as the Great Spirit has gifted us with intelligence, in us also dwells the gift of empathy that wishes life to live harmoniously upon the Illahee's lands that surround us.

"We must conform to the rituals of the High Spirits and be assured that our acceptance is acknowledged by the Saghalie Tyee.

Or, as the days that pass before us grow long and dark, the shadow of our misdeeds shall be cast before our brothers that will one day arrive to witness our sorrowful attempt in justifying our worth before them. Our brothers shall then find our souls justly expelled and sent to our unaccompanied drift to dwell among the kingdoms of the Mesahchie Tahmahnawis' most dire hides."

Chapter 14
Multnomah

"It was a sad day long ago," stated my father to me as we sat before the night's fire.

He told me of the story shared of our brothers, the Wasco, of the first days when waters fell from high above the cliff that is named Multnomah.

"Long ago before even my father's father father's birth, there was a great chioef of the Multnomah that had lost all his sons as they ventured far from our beliefs and chose the Mesahchie Tahmahanawis' evil ways.

My father told me that the chief's sons eyes were red with hate, and they chose to hear the drum beats dof the call to battle aginst their own brothers that lived far from their village.

Given to battle each of the chiewf's sons soon surrendered their souls upon the lands of the Hyas Pishpish, and beneath the Hyas Telecasit, high peak, and it is there that now lie stained their lifeless bodies without heart and lost to their souls.

As Otelagh passes overhead and the moon rises from behind her cloak, can still be heard the calling of the Bad Spirit as he wishes to devour the lost souls that once stood proud and strong amongst our peoples that have now been given to their expulsion beside us.

The chief had lived through many seasons and had only one child remaining to sit beside him, a beautiful daughter.

As he wished to have grandchildren the chief traveled to many villages until he found a young chief that ruled over the Clatsops, and to him, he offered his daughter, and to them, he hoped to share in the joys of their children.

Once the new leaves returned to the sticks arms, and the snows upon the highest peaks had fled to the rivers that pour beneath them, came a great ceremony that brought peoples from many villages from afar to honor their marriage.

The ceremony lasted through several days, and there were canoe races that lasted well into the darkness of night, and horse races began in the early hours of the morning as Otelagh first shone his warmth upon their camp. Bow and arrow tournaments brought out the best of our young braves as they placed their targets further than ever before, and all these gatherings were enjoyed by feasts and dances before the fires of their camp.

The ceremony was the largest to be joined by so many villages from the south and from along the river's course from the east. These were the days that shared the bounty of respect and love for both, the chief of the Clatsop and the daughter of the Chief of the Multnomah.

As quickly as the pointed wings of the swiftest kulakula, bird, drops from the heavens onto its prey, first fell the young children from disease, and then in order of their age and strengths, those peoples too then died without honor.

Through all the tribe's camps that rested beside the

Multnomah's village could be heard wails from those women that still lived through that first day.

It was a day saddened with death and without hope!

All those that still survived thouth the Great Spirit was angry as so many of their friends and family had been taken without cause.

It appeared that the Great Spirit was maddened beyond what they had ever seen, and as the Great Chief gathered his braves and medicine men, he asked them all what they should do to bring happiness before the High Spirit's chair once more?

As silent as snow falling at one's feet stood all that gathered before the chief, all but one old medicine man that stood up and scolded everyone for not accepting death with honor when once faced with the unknownst of what today has brought, and to what tomorrow may place upon all our tables.

As everyone stood and listened to the medicine man's thoughts, they all agreed. But as they too fell silent the oldest medicine man of their village appeared as he came down from the high mountains, not to join in the village's celebration as the Great Chief had asked of him, but to find cure for this sickness that had now swept through all their camps and had taken so many of their brothers and sisters.

The old medicine man, leaning on his walking stick, with calm voice, began to share a secret that his father had shared with him long ago;

"I am an old man and have lived through many suns and moons, and as I stand before you today you will soon know of why I yet survive before you.

"My father too was a great medicine man of our peoples, when he too was at my age he told me that when I would be near his own years a great sickness would fall upon our peoples from the High Spirit.

He stated: "My father told that all those that joined the celebration would die unless a great sacrifice was offered before the Great Spirit's chair."

He told that only a beautiful and innocent maiden from our village, a daughter of a chief, must choose to give her life so that her peoples would survive the disease.

The medicine man stated: "Alone she must go to a high cliff above Big River and throw herself upon the jagged stones below. If she does this, the sickness shall quickly disappear and those that still live shall once again prosper without fear."

As he finished telling of his story he feebly sat before them and told them that now they had heard his secret that he could die in peace.

Soon the chief stood up and as he thought of the medicine man's story, he began to speak to all those present, and he demanded that they bring before him the maidens whos fathers and grandfathers had once been chief to their villages.

Quickly, they all walked away and began to return with 12 young maidens, the Great Chief's daughter too stood before them as she was the most beautiful. Fear and dread approached the Great Chief's heart as he told the story shared by the old medicine man. He hoped that another maiden would step forward to save their nation from further pestilence and death from the hands of the Great Spirit, and that his daughter's life would be spared.

He told the maidens that he too believed in the old medicine man's story, and the vision that he had spoken would again offer life to all those that yet survived the disease.

Then, suddenly, the chief turned to the old medicine man and to his own braves and told them to tell everyone to prepare to die with dignity and with honor, as there would not be a sacrifice allowed by one of their maidens to the High Spirit's wish.

As the chief stood and turned he left all those that were yet sitting to think alone to their thoughts, and the meeting was finished without a further question as to why the chief had changed his decision.

Denying the medicine man's story the villagers continued to fall ill and perish before the brothers and sisters, fathers and mothers, and as the chief's daughter saw all the people of her village and of those that had joined their ceremony, she began to believe that if it were not for her own sacrifice, then who would save those still fortunate to be alive?

But she wanted to live, as she loved her husband deeply, she passed on the thought and continued to help those in their suffering.

A few days had passed since she had first heard of the medicine man's story, and on that morning she saw the sickness appear on her lover's face. She knew instantly what she must do, and as she decided that it was her choice alone to allow all the remaining members of their peoples to live, she cooled her new nusband's face with a wet skin, while she overlooked his grave condition, she then placed a bowl of water beside his bedside, and was then seen no more amongst the village's people.

All that night throughout the next day she walked along the river's course until she reached the high cliff where one could see the kingdom of all the Land's of Wah that stretched from the Great River to the lands of Pahto and Wy-East.

As Otelagh fell from the heavens the chief's daughter stood upon the high cliff and peered down upon the jagged stones that were lain at the foot of what is now Multnomah, and as she raised her arms and knelt onto the ground she wailed to the High Spirit and pleaded for her new lover's life to be spared. She asked; "Are you angry with my people? Will you make the sickness pass if I offer you my life and jump from this high place? Only love and peace and purity I hold within my heart, if you will accept me as the sacrifice that you have spoken, let some token hang in the sky. Allow me to know that my sacrifice will not be unknown and in vain, and that the sickness that you have allowed to take many from our villages will quickly pass."

Given her last words as she wailed unto the heavens, the moon shone bright through the trees from across the Big River. She took this to be the sign that she had asked, and at that very moment as she had promised the High Spirit, she opened her arms to the heavens and screamed out her lover's name and wailed her love to him across the Chinook winds that then began to rush upon her.

And she was taken instantly by the High Spirit to her new village . . .

Otelagh passed overhead the following day, and to the amazement of those that still had strength and were free from the disease those that were stricken ill then stood up from their beds and were cured.

The village's drums spread the word that the sickness had passed along the river's course, to the east and to the west the drum's message could be heard.

Upon the sickness leaving those that had been stricken, all the villagers then began to dance before the Good Spirit and offered thanks for the return of life as they had known it from their first day upon the Hyas Tumtum's creation.

Then, there was silence, a great hush came over the camp, and the question was asked to why the sickness had passed?

The chief thought hard to the question and he again summoned before him the same 12 maidens, and as they stood before him, he noticed, that all were there, but one.

A woman of the village was then heard to ask, "Did one of the maidens stand brave before all their peoples and to the Hyas Tahmahnawis and jump from the high cliff?"

The young Clatsop chief turned from the meeting and began to run along the trail to the Big River, and many others followed in his fast steps as they too wanted to know if it were to be true that the Chief's daughter had sacrificed her life and breath new life into them so that they would not perish.

Their group approached the rocks that were lain at the bottom of the High Cliff, and with saddened eyes they began to weep, as there, speared to the jagged stones, lay the chief's lifeless body.

It was at that place they decided to honor her gift to them all, and she was placed beneath the soils of the earth where her spirit would live on for all the suns and moons to pass overhead.

Her father, the Great Chief, knelt beside her grave as he too wailed before them and pleaded for them to honor her bravery and courage, and for them to show him some sign that her death was not in vain, and that her soul would lie entombed beside their own chairs.

Suddenly, all eyes were pointed to the heavens and toward the highest rock of the cliff, and soon a stream of silvery white water began to fall from over the cliff's edge. The waters began to break apart and suddenly turned into a fine mist before it again gathered and fell at their feet. The water's stream continued to float down upon them and as they stood in approval of the High Spirit's gift, they all agreed to name this new Tumwater, The Mulnomah Falls.

From that first day the waters have fallen from the high cliff and into its deep pool, and as the new leaves have since fallen from their hosting sticks branching arms, and the young of the mowitch and loolack are not seen in the meadows, and the young of the Kalakala have begun to fly to waters distant to our own, the young warrior and chief stands in grief beside his beautiful bride at the site of her grave.

Here you may see her dressed in white along one side of Multnomah's cliff at the edge of the sticks as she views the place where she stood stronger and more courageous than all her people's combined as she gave sacrifice to her heart to the High Spirit.

But her soul lives on amongst us all as we stand below Mulnomah's fall, and know that her sacrifice has allowed us all to live free from fear to the power that the Hyas Tahmahnawis' had allowed to spread by his most dire wish . . .

Chapter 15
Crow Spirit

With watchful eyes Kahkah, Crow sees all.

The Hyas Spirit, Tumtum, long ago took from the Earth when Sun first rose upon the horizon, burnt ash from the fires expelled from the bellies of the fathers and mothers of Wy-East, Pahto, and Lawala Clough that are now named the Tkope Lemoto, Goat Rocks. With water he placed them into a great bowl, and as he mixed the dark ash with water that fell from the heavens as Otelagh wept upon his passing overhead, the form of Crow was molded for all life to share.

Hyas Tumtum then gave Crow wings with which to fly above all the lands of his creation, and once Crow stood on his own upon the highest branch overlooking the kingdoms of the illahee, our Hyas Tumtum asked only of Crow to cleanse the lands of disease and death, and to lead those unwary to what danger looms beyond the unsightless journey's of their travels across his kingdoms to safely flee through Crow's most raucous and leading call.

Crow Spirit has great powers!

Crow Spirit can deliver us both into or far from the hungered mouths of the Bad Spirits.

Tumtum gave our peoples the gift of intelligence in order that we have choices in our lives, and in those choices it is only ourselves that can be blamed when we do not heed the call of Crow to gather below his tireless shielding wing.

With the wisdom of Crow above me, and with the cunning of Coyote beside me, I should go far in my travels below the guidance of our Hyas Tumtum, and by the light spread across my path by Otelagh's passing reign, my journey amongst our peoples shall always be illuminated for all to follow . . .

Chapter 16
Wahkeena's Gift

As I have lain conquest to Multnomah's crown and have witnessed the immaculacy of Multnomah's words, I have traversed through the trees of the Wah's forest as the High Spirit's voices resonate within my soul, yet they do not lend their voices to the Great Chinook as it passes above me as I near the grounds that our Princess Wahkeena has been honored.

As the creek of Multnomah has long disappeared into the valley below the trail, I have succeeded in securing my presence upon the beginning of Wah's most highly respected angelic grounds.

I have descended from the trail's peak and have approached the grounds that hold the Spirits that blend their forms within the waters that lead to the land of Wahkeena. I have found myself entering a kingdom mixed with warm light cast across its banks, and

Wahkeena's waters are engaging through the beauty of her cascade's graceful slide from above me as it twists and turns to the river below. As I stand amidst her presence, the Spirit to which she bears true has chosen to share the story of Wahkeena's proven placement upon these most generous grounds.

"It was many years ago that Wahkeena one day chose to walk far from her village to visit a young brave, Two Fists, of the Nehalem Village. His village stands upon the banks of another great river that leads to the Great Waters of the setting sun, and they too, alike our own peoples, lay their nets within the river and take from it pish that return home and breathe new life to all species that rise from the soils that surround it.

Wahkeena had first joined a great ceremony honoring the village of the Nehalem for their culling of a large whale as it had neared the shore of the Great Waters and offered its soul for food to sustain them through the rains and cold of the approaching winter. One evening, as many villages joined together and began to thank the Great Spirit for the gift of this whale, Wahkeena was approached by Two Fists as they would then sit before the great fire and speak of their families and of themselves.

As the night grew long and their eyes did not drift far from one another they were smiled upon by many of the village's guests as they passed by their gathering. It has been told that the air above and surrounding Wahkeena and Two Fists was thick with passion, and that all knew that one day they both would join before the gathering of their villages and become one with one another and to the Earth.

Many days passed as the ceremony had ended and Wahkeena had not heard word from Two Fists. She feared that she had mislain her heart before him and that he had chose another woman to share his life. Wahkeena asked to where he was and to what he had been doing and everyone that she had spoken to had no answer for her that offered calm to her heart and hope for her soul.

As the darkness of winter's clouding drew heavy on her heart, time passed slowly for Wahkeena. She mourned each day, each minute that she was seperated from her handsome Brave. Yet, there was no answer from Two Fist's tribe, or from Two Fists himself.

Then one day as Wahkeena sat below the beauty of Multnomah's fall and thought of the story of how it came to be long ago when disease swept through many tribes and took many brothers and sisters from their sides. Wahkeena had then felt the love that the chief of the Multnomah's daughter had felt for the brave from the Clatsop tribe as she selflessly chose to give her life so that he and all that yet survived the disease may live once again without fear.

Wahkeena chose to walk beyond the high cliffs of Multnomah with tears in her eyes until she reached the fast waters that raced beside her feet, and then suddenly, without pause or concernment, a voice from high above where she stood called out."

"Wahkeena, I know your heart is with Two Fists, but you must know that his soul has been taken from him by the Bad Spirit that dwells amongst the fast waters of the river that passes Two Fist's village. You should not grieve his absence, but be proud that you each had the moments you had shared. Two Fists' spirit has now been taken to the waters where each season is drawn from its depths the spirits of the Salmon as they once again arrive to their home waters to offer life to renew surrounding them. If it were not for his love for you he would not emerge and be seen as the Fish that leads his school before you as we would not have taken him from the Bad Spirit's purse and made offer for his soul to give life for all the days and moons that shall pass from this day on."

"As Wahkeena listened intently to the Great Spirit's spoken words she rose up from the soils where she had sat and climbed to the top of the slope where the fast waters begin their plunge to the river.

As she overlooked the grounds that stood below her, she opened her arms and wailed unto the heaven to the High Spirits so that they would take the curls from her hair and lay them upon the course of the stream.

Wahkeena asked that the flowers that rose up beside Two Fists and herself as they sat together that single, most remarkable night would too rise from these grounds and line the stream's banks with their sweet scent as they each would call out his name and welcome Two Fists upon his journey's return to her side.

"Many, many long days passed Wahkeena as she sat lonely along the stream's bank and awaited Two Fists return, and sadly, one day, her heart was beyond approach and her soul laden with hurt and she was taken from the physical to the spirit world.

"These are the grounds that you now enter Nenamooks, you have chanced upon the princess of these lands as her array lies tenuously curled amongst the water's curtaining form, and you have entered into the property that is hailed as the land of our alluring Wahkeena.

"You shall find that her grounds have been chosen to your immediate and convincing response as her spirit is convincingly discovered seductive to your entrance.

"Wahkeena is blessed throughout her surroundings with bouquets of flowers spread beyond the curvaceous banks of her stream that is certain to denote of her royalty to all those that stand upon her grounds. Each bouquet, each flower, each petal perform their unending and swaying dance as it is correlated by Wahkeena's most sensuous and beckoning breaths, as she is now tasked in her delivery to again lure Two Fists to her side.

"Nenamooks, this is how this property so named for Wahkeena had begun. Throughout her life after she had met Two Fists she had not lost faith or hope, and through her strength and endurance we all can learn of her spirit.

Teach your peoples that we are born of the same Spirit, and that all our brothers must be promised given their life's work as they pass across our lands, and to all the lands that are spread before their winsome path.

"All mankind must accept that their respect of nature is as hallowed as they detect notably within their marriage!

"Take your advice to your peoples and express before them that if they wish to be placed in our Spirit, they must first find the discipline that will allow them to follow the path of righteousness that we committably speak.

"The same lessons that you have gained from your journey were anointed to your father and your father's father before him as they had also established their completion and understanding of our truths. Then, and only then did their lessons allow your people closer to their delivery of our Spirit.

""Mankind was first instituted upon this Earth owning to our individuality, and through our individuality we must also see that in each gift that the Hyas Spirit has blessed upon us that we each must share that same respect and be committed to and married to the gift of life that we have been so honored!

"Mankind must be aware that if they are to build upon the land's of this Earth that they must first become aware to the gifts that are betrothed before them.

"Mankind must be certain that the lands that they build their meager dwellings were indeed meant to be chosen for their accommodation, and not warranted for all mankind to cherish and reap of the land's most revered spiritual rewards as are these very grounds that we now share.

"Look upon our spirit and you shall find the truths of your measure to the people's of the Earth. Be not afraid our son, for we now go destined to our path's unveiling before all mankind if you choose to endorse the bounties of our harvest and lead our peoples toward their marriage unto the heavens."

I firmly understand that I must become involved with all my tribe and of all those that are chosen to their stay upon the soil's of the earth. As the significance of our Spirit's guidance shall accommodate the poise of my peoples complete, and their claim one day as the guardians to these lands shall then appear before them.

I must be tuned to my brother's successes before the Great Spirits and allow our peoples of their rewarding placement before all mankind!

We, the members of the tribe of Watlalla shall be accepted as the caretakers of these lands.

May our marriages be heralded to the heavens and the Earth alike, and may our labors be fruitful to those that choose upon our traces as they venture further upon the trails that we now share.

As we become the Spirits unto all the Land's of Wah and within The Valley Of The Eagle, we all may one day be discovered of our soar upon the winds permitted by the authority created by our spirited souls.

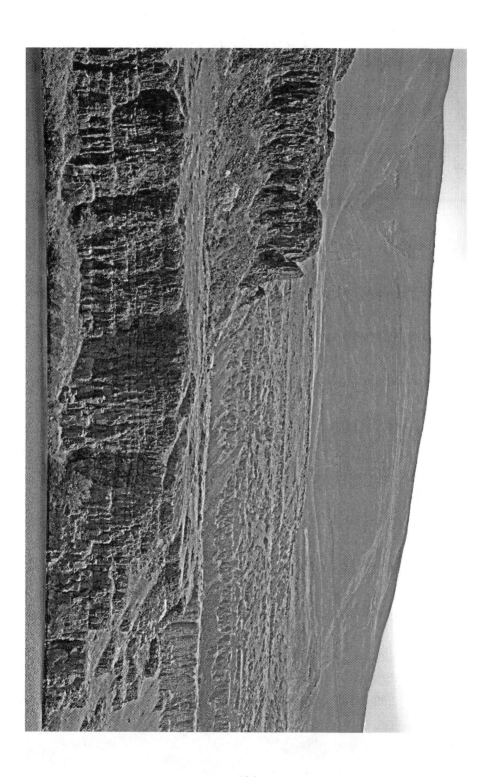

Chapter 17
Our Brothers of the Wisscopam

My Great Father, Mokst Tahmahnawis, has now completed his journey upon our Illahee and now soars across the heavens with our Hyas Spirits.

I have seen his trail streak before me every evening that I have sat before the fire of my camp as I recaptured the many talks that we shared. He is always sitting next to me in spirit, and in that spirit I have chosen to follow his lead and direction in our people's course as my father's spirits had led him.

One day a brother from the south where the great Waku-nunee-Tuki, Mt. Shasta draws its breath sat before our fires and spread the words that soon there would be many of our brothers lost to the Bad Spirit. He shared that the Hyas Spirits would be displeased with their foundering and that as I was the son of Mokst Tahmahnawis, and the Chief of the Watlalla, that I should speak to the Hyas Spirits and ask for their guidance before our own misguided brothers accepted the Mesahchie Tahmahnawis' invitation to stand upon his own desecrated grounds.

It was upon the Hyas Spirit's guide that I began my march through the Land's of Wah and was led along the banks of the Great River, and it was upon this very trail that my leaders had determined I was to be remarked toward the responsibility of my quest.

The good spirits have stated that I would find solitude amongst the Hyas Trees as I walked beneath their reverence, and that their swaying shall allow my enrichment in the gifts of patience and of fortitude that would enable me to overcome the turbulence and influence that the Mesahchie Tahmahnawis had tethered to our distant brother's misguided souls.

Our Kloshe Tahmahnawis had acknowledged that as the notes of wisdom are dispersed by the Chinook's calming breeze and influences our brother's spirits, our wisdom shall then bring harmony and respect to all that resist the angry soul of the Bad Spirit's futile temptations.

These immortal Lands of Wah had given me support throughout the suns and moons of my rule before my peoples, and as I neared the beginning of the trail that leads to our brothers of the Wisscopam I began a journey where only the teachings of the Good Spirits should be determined before my brothers.

If I did not concede to the Evil Spirit's persistence for my soul, my quest shall be safely purported as I strive to stand in my forefathers footsteps and cling to their dreams of mankind's abstinence from the battles that are wrought by our own disregard for life's treasure!

Mankind shall live and prosper throughout the suns and moons of my reign before them, just as have all my brothers that have knelt before the water's of Wahclella.

I had journeyed before the Council of Wahclella many times to clasp the hands that have provided our peoples with the intelligence to adhere fortitude and principle toward the days that rise before us, and as we have retained and held rigid to these gifts, they have allowed our esteem before all peoples.

I must share my vision before all others that I pass and speak in that I had seen our peoples, all peoples of this great land living beneath our heaven, our numbers strong as are the stars that are spread from one side to the other across the horizons. We must grasp hands, and in that bond we shall remain strong and fear not the advance of the Mesachie Tawmahnawis for our souls.

My vision has lain a message of truth and understanding in that if we, the peoples of this Illahee stand proud and strong, and vigilant and observing before all life's trepidations, we shall be seen by the Hyas Tahmahnawis as one nation and not many men of many nations.

We must all grasp to the importance that life brings before us all and we must agree and understand that we are each as one. In that, we shall defeat those others that wish to instill fear within our souls and blacken our hearts as their souls have been taken from them, and in turn we shall find prosperity and privilege upon the soils that the Hyas Sun spreads his warming hand above us all.

As I had accepted the Spirit's wishes I began to journey through the lands that border the great water that lead to our brothers of the Wisscopam who have taken refuge upon the site where they catch the spirits of Quenett, Trout, at WinQuatt, place encircled by bold cliffs: "The Dalles, Oregon"

I have travelled to this village once before as I had surveyed the lands that rise beneath the dawning Otelagh, Sun, and to the mountains that hold the Oluk, Snake, that our brothers of the Nez Perz are to be found.

I remember the illahee, land, that the Wisscopam occupied was void of the Hyas Sticks that are many within the Lands of Wah, and that many Sail Sticks, Cottonwoods were gathered upon the banks that hold the Hyas Tamolitsh, Great Bucket of Fast Waters, from approach to the Wisscopam's village.

As I sit before the fire within the lodge of Hyak Leloo, Swift Wolf, and find myself engaged by our conference to the problems that have now arose before our brothers, I was told by Hyak Leloo that as I travelled through the lands of our country even though the Spirits would exhale the frozen breaths of winter, the snow would fall silent upon the grounds that lie before me, and that if I were to sit quietly and listen to their voice that settle from these same breaths that I may hear the heartbeats that promise life to abound upon our lands.

Within those same heartbeats, Swift Wolf stated, I may find triumph in alluring our brother's baffling conduct from the Mesahchie Tahmahnawis, and if I were to fail to discover the Hyas Spirits directives and convince our brothers from their errors that it shall one day allow the Bad Spirit to hail from upon the highest telocaset, mountaintop.

Swift Wolf also stated that the Mesahchie Tahmahnawis would then cast his indifference over our surviving brothers that still contest to his gruesome reign upon our Earth, and that he would then be known to rule the Illahee from upon the mounts of the ghastly boneyards wrought by those that stood oppressed to the Saghalie Tyhee's wishes.

May our souls resist the temptations that may be soon cast before us!

The afternoon has passed swiftly as Hyak Leloo and I had been taken thoroughly through the course of Sun above us as it has spread its light upon our peoples. Hyak Leloo and I have agreed to stand before our brothers and share the reasoning behind the urgency of our trek, and through our counsel, we shall ask our brothers to expell the bad thoughts and deeds that the Bad Spirit spreads amongst us, and administer their weighty souls legitimately toward the mannerisms that the Good Spirit pleads.

As the tenas polaklie otelagh, evening sun, has begun to plunge behind the mountains across the great water we have gathered before the fire of the Chief of the Wisscopam named Tyee Kahkwa Klale, Chief Blackfish.

This formidable leader to his peoples, and Swift Wolf and I, have taken the souls of Metlako's treasures from above the flame of our fire and have begun to feast.

We have elected to adjourn our speech until the brothers of this village have once again gathered before the camp's fire as we then shall examine our distinctiveness upon this Illahee that our mortal souls are drawn.

A cold, silvery moon has risen above the stick's highest peaks and the tribe of these high cliffs have gathered before the fire of their camp. As their chief had requested, they have all sat quietly with anticipation and have awaited the talks that will give reason for my arrival before them.

Chief Blackfish had stated earlier as we first sat before our feast that he too had encountered a vision of this day's arrival, and that he had also seen the battles of our peoples as they were scoured throughout the properties that the Mesahchie Tahmahnawis hails.

We had fed our hungry bellies until we could not continue, and as Chief Blackfish rose before the peoples of his village he has begun to address the issues that have been brought before his table.

"My peoples, we are gathered before the fire this night as a brother and the Chief of the Watlalla that has been chosen by the Kloshe Tahmahnawis must now take upon our forefathers trail across the lands of our Illahee and pretend before the Mesahchie Tahmahnawis' ruse. He must distract our brothers from their foolishness as they have promised to battle alongside the Bad Spirit as they are lured within the captived chambers that expels all life from existing within *their grasp as the darkness of their souls allows the chill of the winter to be drawn unto them.*

We have all heard the pathetic screams that have been burdened within the breaths of the Chinook as it has blown across our lands, and as these screams awake us from our sleep we must now give our allegiance to Nenamook's reference as the Good Spirits have requested."

As I stand before my brothers of the Wisscopam I find myself strengthened by the Chief's announcement pertaining to my arrival within their village, and as I stand proudly before their numbers I began to speak of our Forfather's wishes;

"Klahowya!

My brothers of the Wisscopam.

My Brothers, may we all live in peace and harmony throughout the emergence of the dawning light that gives life to all the species that thrive upon the Saghalie Tyee's conception! May our own species be revived from our misguided characteristics and be discovered trustworthy in our beliefs as we subject our philosophical understanding towards the teachings that the Council has dispersed through me, and may these teachings take our own Spirit aloft into the heavens from the seditious depths of the Illahee that the Mesahchie Tahmahnawis has declared solely as his own!

May the irreverent spirit be treasured below our commission upon our Illahee, and may his attempts of defiance and degradation upon the soils above his reign be lessened as we find ourselves appalled at his ployful and subjective behavior!

The day has arrived for the elders of our nation to trek throughout the lands of this nation, and as we are found marching to the homelands of our brothers that we have not yet stood, we shall be seen as prophets of humanity before them.

Our brothers shall surely take notice that their adjournment from upon this Earth and before the gates of their Spirits shall not be met if they do not accomodate the teachings that we have promised to lie out before them.

My brothers, we all must succeed in alluring our peoples from their stray, and as we gather their numbers to follow in our paths, mankind shall be survived by the qualities that have allowed our Spirits to stand announced upon the Walls of Wahclella that rise mightily within the lands where great waters fall from the heavens.

Our fathers have found honor before their fathers as their passage has been accepted by the Kloshe Tahmahnawis, and as they have proudly taken their stance before me. They too have promised that we can discover the Sacred Trail of Truths within our souls that will allow us, alike the Hyas Spirits, to stand proud upon the lands that they have once led.

It is now our lead to righteousness that will admit us honorably to one day find our stance upon the Walls of Wahclella by our forfather's selection!

Long ago the Saghalie Tyee had formed alliance with the Great Spirit of the Earth to allow all the peoples of this Illahee to wander freely within the avenues of their individuality. The Saghalie Tyee has given us both the path that teaches us the wisdom of the Good Spirit, and the Saghalie Tyee has also allowed our brothers to follow the path that allows our blinded souls to become labored and lost by the Bad Spirit's guise as it separates our brothers and ourselves from attaining peace and harmony amongst all the lands that comprise the gift that our Illahee was first chosen!

Many of our brothers have now sadly taken the trail that is owned by the Tahkenitch, Many Arms, of the Mesahchie Tahmahnawis and are lost to our peoples forever!

The doctrine that I have been encouraged to spread before our peoples are comprised of the explicit principles that the Saghalie Tyee had wished that we would not find our objection, and it is our distant brothers that we find siding with the Mesahchie Tahmahnawis that fear to sit patient and wait for the passing of the Mesahchie Tahmahnawis' storm that will not abide by these principles.

It shall be those same brothers that will not find their step again upon the trails that are soon to be sadly strewn before us!

May our remaining brothers listen to the words of reason as they are cast throughout the lands by the breaths of the Great Chinook, and may their souls resist the temptations that the Mesahchie Tahmahnawis shall expel alluringly before them!

I ask of you all, who may stand beside me and deliver this message before our brothers across the lands that will soon unfold before us?

Mitlite nesika kahpho chako chitish, pe klaska tenas chako chope kopakonaway okoke otelagh pe moon kopa klatawa kimtah!

May our sisters become grandmothers, and their sons become grandfathers for all the suns and moons to follow!

Due to the profession that has been wrought before my family by the Hyas Spirits upon these great lands, I, Nenamooks, the Chief of the Watlalla and the son of the great Chief Mokst Tahjmahnawis, has also chosen to become tethered upon the trails that lead from my village and approach the distant properties that our Illahee clasps.

I too stand as a mere mortal before the Great Spirits as do you all my brothers that have been welcomed before the fires of my camps, and by the teachings and my petitioning by the Hyas Spirits, I must distinguish myself before all the peoples of this Earth and to the spirits that inhabit and rise from beneath the fissures of our lands. I must share the philosophies that the Saghalie Tyee has tersed as I have stood compliant to his lecture before the Hallowed Walls and beneath the Pillars of Candor that stand polished upon the closure to the Trail of Principles.

It is upon the Great Rock that stands above the plunge of the Hyas Waters that the teachings by the Council of Wahclella have been dispersed to all the Chiefs of our peoples, and as I too have knelt before their presence, they have challenged me to gather the chiefs of the Chinook and have challenged those of our brothers that choose to follow in their request to trek across the soils of this Earth.

The Hyas Spirits have demanded that we summon righteousness to again prevail throughout our lands as we necessitate a peaceful closure toward all misunderstandings that our brothers have become challenged. Our brothers must believe that we have the wish spiked within our souls to once again clutch respect and share dignity before all life that flourishes upon our Illahee as we were bore to exhibit given the days of our beginnings.

The Council has stated; "As the peoples of this Earth accepts peace between one another's tribes, it shall then be promised that our brothers shall conquer the Mesahchie Tahmahnawis' intemperance for humanities salvation that he unsparingly and direly spreads."

I have been told of wars brought forth from the greed of our brothers and that they had quickly found their battle lost, as their lives were sacrificed and presented before the Mesahchie Spirit and were then thrust beneath to the catacombs of his reign.

It has been discovered that this spirit has now extinguished the life upon the lands that gave reason for our brother's survival upon them, and we must not dare our souls to trace across these barren lands as the mighty Pishpish lie in wait for their spiritless quarry.

I have met many brothers as I had traversed across their paths, and many have joined my side as brothers to this Illahee and have decreed to satisfy their thirst and hunger through the words that our Saghalie Tyee has shared.

"Nika Ows, Nika Tillikums. Kloshe tumtum mika chako kopa okoke nesika siwash house!

My Brothers, My Peoples. Welcome to our lodge!"

As we are now encircled before the flame that gives marrow to our existence we must distinguish the teachings of our great brothers that have passed into the cole Illahee, winters, of their lives.

These great brothers, the Spirits of our Great Nation of the Chinook, the Spirits that embrace our Hyas Illahee and give hope to our peoples so we may grasp the importance of their wisdom and not perish by the misdeeds of the Mesahchie Tahmahnawis have directed the highest precedence for our potlatch, meeting.

As my father had once taken his stance before the Council of Wahclella, I too have knelt before their counsel as I have enlightened my peoples toward the vigilance of the Hyas Tahmahnawis' direction. As I knelt worshiping upon the rock high above the water's stream my soul had silently passed through the water's rush to the Great

River and my plea before the Council had been dispersed before their Hallowed Walls.

As I knelt before our Spirit's compelling review and was consumed by their principles they again rewarded my request for their escort through the toils of my decisions.

Upon my acceptance before our Hyas Brother's inquiry I quickly became zealous before their counsel, and as I stood challenged before their review, they have requested that I once again gather the Chiefs that thrive within our great nation and have asked me to spell upon your souls the message that shall again prove upon our people's acceptance to the morality of our Saghalie Tyee's ideals.

The High Council that Wahclella is solemnly bound has lain a message that must be dispersed before all the Illahee's peoples. My brothers, as we are attuned to the Spirit's teachings we must be adamant upon their request.

As I sit before you, I must instill the wisdom of our Spirit's words to lie deep within your souls. As you digest the decree of the images that they have spelled before us through my eyes, I know we shall all be traced throughout the trails of our Illahee's lands as we acknowledge our Spirit's wishes.

We will determine that our tasks as they are lain ahead shall be found confidently evident by our efforts, and our brothers shall be granted their estimable tenure upon our Hyas Illahee as it may then become favorably apparent that our souls shall one day be reconnected to their image.

If the wealth of your own spirit is rewarded you by your journey alonside me by the Hyas Tahmahnawis, then it will also ascertain your soul to be provocatively bound by the wisdom of your character!

My brothers, the Great Chiefs of our nation appeared upon the hardened stone of Wahclella's face, and as their features emanated unopposed to the gravity of their station, they have stated that the leaders of all the nations that adhere to the soils of this Earth must unite and give promise that the fuel that breeds the blaze of anger, and persuades the advent of death to devastate the doorways of our lives, must be extinguished and secured once again with respect and dignity that humanity was first drawn to exhibit.

The High Counsel of Wahclella empowered the clouds that were tethered to the skies to unfold above me as Sun rose upon us, and as Sun toured the avenues of the heavens overhead the Great Spirits allowed me to journey through the fleeting suns and moons that our Illahee has maneuvered. I was confused by man's behavior toward one anothers peoples as I observed the deceptive and bloody onslaughts that we have savagely allowed.

As I sat horrified by the unforgivable scores of treachery and treason that our brothers have lain upon one another's peoples, I quickly understand the necessity of this teaching as our peoples must not compliment the disputes of our neighbors, but we must disclose our character unclouded to the treachery that is now seen inherent throughout our lands and toward the brothers that are now found lying and stained upon our Illahee's grounds.

As the suns and moons have long passed since the day that my father stood before our brotherhood, we have now entered into a spell wrought by the Bad Spirit when our brothers are promised to the cadence of the Bad Spirit's drum. If you listen to the winds you may hear their dance before the evening's fires of their camps as they wantonly dance to the rythym of the battles that they have now pledged.

In their dance they have not only promised to spill upon the soils the blood of their brothers, but they have unknowingly chosen to become lost to their own soul's keep.

The Mesahchie Tahmahnawis that lives amongst us has chosen to confuse our souls with its own disorder, and it has begun to undermine all the labors that our brothers have promised to perform before the Kloshe Tahmahnawis.

Our brothers are now dispersed to the lands of their neighbors with fire shackled within their eyes, and we, the guardians that preside within the Great Nation of the Chinook must once again term the distinctness of our humanity before our brothers and attack the disharmony the Bad Spirit has provokingly endorsed.

Remember my brothers, that as you reacquant our brothers to the order and specificity of humanity, you must also make our brothers aware of the complaint that the Mesahchie Tahmahnawis reeks upon all our souls!

The Great Spirits have stated that as our presence is turned from the western waters of our beginnings and are spread throughout all the mountains and plains of our Illahee, we will find that our brothers have joined with separate Spirits that pledge upon their lives, and though their Tahmahnawis' may be disclosed by a differing title, in this, we shall find no cause for war brought forth by our brother's difference and of their customs.

We must become considered toward the Great Spirits that are all bound to the Earth as they allow strength to be bred to the peoples that live beneath their reign!

There are many tribes that are spread upon the soils of our Illahee, and many distinctions of these tribes are to be discovered beyond the reaches of our strides.

As our brothers are promised upon earth to be associated as our equals, they must be allowed to lead their lives by the teachings of their Good Spirits.

We must believe that our brother's measure upon this Illahee is adjusted by the Great Spirit as is ours.

As our brother's laborious efforts are performed daily as their Spirit's teachings commit, our brothers shall also upon the day of their Saghalie Tyee's choosing be led either to the gates promised to the kingdom before their Kloshe Tahmahnawis or be led to the vanquished grounds of their Mesahchie Tahmahnawis.

It is the good and the bad of our own spirit that we and our brothers must be judged, and not by the differences specifically wrought by the Spirits that live amongst us, or the grounds that we live, or by the riches that lie beneath our villages that we are fortunately credited.

Our brothers must all be permitted the treasures that our Illahee offers, and of these treasures we must not permit the wars of our encampments to become associated by our greed for their unharmonious ransom.

My brothers!

We must all strive to accept the wisdom permitted by our brother's spirits, and as all the brothers of our Illahee are found accomplished by the Hyas Tahmahnawis' teachings, we may then command the greatest gift chosen for mankind's cradle.

The gift of peace between our brother's tribes that are offered by our Kloshe Tahmahnawis is alike the Earth's shadow as it is seen raised from the darkened features that our moon shares, and as our humanitarian campaign brings illumination to our worth before all man, our compliance to the Hyas Tahmahnawis' principles shall persuade the entirety of our brother's aberrations to flee from the grasp of the Mesahchie Tahmahnawis.

Through the innocence of our gift, all humanity may then be discovered consummate by our own formidable and notable existence, and our bright path upon Earth shall be seen secured if our peoples determine to accept the ethics that our Forfathers have placed impeccably upon our table.

May our paths meet once again before the Spirit of the winter is lain upon all our tomorrows, and may the wisdom that these philosophies bare keep you safeguarded from the disease that the Mesahchie Tahmahnawis so willingly spreads from within its darkened purse!"

Chapter 18

The Silenced Breaths of the Smoke Spirits

This is my trial before the Hyas Tahmahnawis as he led me along the Great River and towards the Great Waters of the mamook otelagh, setting sun, and it was along this shoreline of the great river that my journey allowed me to become afoot without a vision from the High Spirit.

A test was thrust before me by the High Spirits as I stepped quickly from amongst songs shared by the kalakalas, birds, and then, quickly, their beautiful chorus fell silent as it was spilled upon deaf ears by the emergence of the Smoke Spirits, Fog Spirits.

I had found myself grasping to every note that fell from above me as the sun shone my way along the trail that the spirits led, and it was upon this same trail that I discovered my soul suddenly wavering amongst the fog that quickly hid the spirits of every tupso, grass, and stick, tree, that grew upon the trail chosen of my journey.

I first stood tall as I walked amongst the light cast by the Hyas Illahee Tumtum, the Great Earth Spirit, Sun. I learned through this lesson wrought by the Tahmahnawis that I was only a leader to my peoples when light was spread across my path as I could only then foresee the trails that would lead to the heaven's treasured paths.

As I was called upon by the Tahmahnawis from within the cold and dark cast of the smoke as it was spread thick upon me, I found myself weakened as I knelt before the judgment of the High Spirit's query.

As the day turned itself to night, I was challenged as a mortal amongst the Great Spirits as the light of day was not cast upon my path!

I lost grasp of my vision's trace given my people's salvation as was directed by the Tahmahnawis upon our earthen trails, as they were then strewn unkept across the lands that I could no longer safely cross!

I stood alone and discouraged as darkness was cast across my path by the Kloshe Tahmahnawis', Good Spirits, and in this darkness, allowed my faith to be easily taken from my grasp as the unknown allowed uncertainty and fear to gather within me as the Skookum Tahmahnawis', Bad Spirits, that our peoples have fled for many suns and moons, then held captive to my own challenged and burdened soul!

I found my efforts to lead my peoples safely through the challenges of our lives, and to stand before the Hyas Tahmahnawis now unfavored.

My soul was then fastened to the lands of the Hyas Pishpish Tahmahnawis, Great Cat Spirit, and was promised to dwell within the dens of the Klale Lolo, Black Bear, if I were not able to once again surrender my own mortality and grasp the sanctity treasured within my spirit.

As the Hyas Tahmahnawis cast my soul across the lands of the Great Cat and toward the dens of the Great Bear within Wy-East's lands, I found myself lost to my error as I could not assure my path through the mire that I had then chose to let mold within me.

My mind lay adrift as if it were a branch as it was quickly swept down the Great Eagle to the Mighty River and beyond to the water's of the setting sun.

My senses had deserted me, and my way upon Earth's trails were quickly lost!

I found fear where trust had once stood proudly, I felt betrayal where loyalty had once been known to flourish!

I prayed for the Hyas Tumtum's direction, and it was then that the silenced breaths of the Smoke Spirits chose my soul to wander aimlessly into the darkened regions that shadows are not cast.

I stood lost and bewildered to my way before the High Spirits!

Upon my place within the Hyas Lolo's den I thought that the spirits had deserted me and not I toward them.

I knew I had no power to yield before our fathers, the chiefs of our peoples, and the Great Spirits that our lands are treasured. I was swept unto the lands beneath Wy-East's delate hyas kloshe telecaset, magnificent mountaintop, the lands now ruled by the hyas ticky pight pe polaklie tumtum of okoke Solleks Tahmahnawis okoke elip ticky mamoock halo saghalie kopa nesika tillikums, fierce and darkened heart of the Angry Spirits that choose ruin upon our peoples.

"Kumtux kopa kwolan, nika, cly, Hyas Tahmahnawis!

"Hear my cry High Spirit!

"Hear my cry to save our peoples from those spirits who rule amidst darkness' most dishonoring reign

"Kumtux kopa kwolan nika cly!"

As silence fell upon my ears and great smoke covered the grounds that I stood, I plead before the High Spirits!

I found myself again afoot without a vision from the High Spirit!

Alone, my pleas fell silently amongst the emptiness of this land's tribe.

Alone I stood.

Unaware to the direction of my step I failed to surrender my mortality and grasp to the strengths that once inhabited my spirited soul!

I stood before all our peoples across all the lands that we have traced as a lost soul without spirit!

In fear!

Without vision!

Without hope!

Without dignity!

Without honor!

I am as a mortal amongst mortals once more!

I remember to the story my grandfather told of stars that fall from the heavens and are scattered across all the lands. Through his teachings, I remember that I must not grasp the tail of those fleeting stars as they fall from the heaven's trails and now lay scattered upon our Illahee, Earth. But, I must gather the strength that these fireballs thrust upon us and give direction to our peoples so that we may also thrive one day upon the trails that survive amongst the gateways highered to our own upon this land.

We must find ourselves honored to our trace upon Earth as we spell of righteousness before the Saghalie Tyee, High God, before the cole wind of nesika cole illahee, cold breaths of our winter arrives upon our lives!

I must resist the darkened hollows of my mortal soul as it now lies wandered throughout all the lands, and I must rise up upon the heaven's gateways and grasp to the strengths that my spirit had once shone brightly!

I must once again regain my vision!

I must once again gain hope!

I must once again find dignity through my vision before the Saghalie Tyee!

I must once again gain honor before my peoples so that they too may resist the tails of those fallen stars that beg for our people's souls to become scattered, and before our people's lives are lain wandered aimlessly across the barren grounds of our Illahee!

I must survive my warning if my peoples are to survive alongside me!

I must find strength within the silence of the Smoke Spirit's baited and frozen breaths, and in that alone, the light from our Great Otelagh shall once again shine and bring warmth to the lands and fill our tables with the souls of the creatures that we desire.

These are my people's stories,

My peoples, held strong by our spirit.

Our spirits, held taut by those Spirits that we are surrounded.

May we be succeeded by many generations before the Hyas Tahmahnawis' gather, and prosper amongst all the kingdoms that they have chose for our survive . . .

Chapter 19
Our People's Commitment

This is the story of my peoples journey far from the Kingdom of Wah upon the trails of our Fathers that now leads to the distant lands of Pahto and Lawala Clough where we are now marked. I am the elder of my peoples, and it was upon the breaths of our Spirits that was announced my name to my witness of their petition far from our village upon the lands of the Tkope Lemoto, White Goat.

Our peoples have now been welcomed for many seasons upon our village's claim, and as the moon begins to rise above the lands, and the Hyas Otelagh was soon to be chosen of his descent, many brothers were now approaching our gathering and spoke of their calling before the Tenas Pahto.

I knew if the Council of the Cascades had spoken to all the brothers that were approaching our village their report before us would bring eminent forewarning to what may soon be looming upon the unpromised horizons of our term beneath

Otelagh's wishes.

As we sat before the fires of our camp and listened to their claim of their summons, I was as bewildered to their witness as I was to the day that the snows that had fallen peacefully upon the highest peaks above our camp had chosen to plunge upon us as the rains surged from upon the Hyas Tumtum's cheeks and emptied into the depths of the Great River.

Our brother's warning of a distant war grew strong as each breath they spoke drew scenes of bloodshed and waste across our kingdoms.

My alarm to what is soon to arrive before us would begin from the lands where Hyas Otelagh first rose, as these were the lands that our brothers had traveled far to seek advice before Pahto's shadow.

I had not met many of these brothers to this day, and they spoke that they were directed to our party by the Hyas Tahmahnawis' point so that I would lead their party to the lands that our peoples were once thrust.

It was told that I alone had been sanctioned to share before all that arrived to our village the righteoused path beyond the guard of the Okope Lemoto, and of our welcome upon the hallowed of grounds that the Land's of Wah bring measure.

To hail such numbers from our brother's camps brings great affliction to my thoughts as I cannot feign to escape its meaning as our brothers have witnessed their distress before us.

It is alike these same numbered tribes that they speak that will fall upon the meadow's glades as they shall be held within its blaze that the Evil Tahmahnawis shall soon be drawn from.

I fear that many of these same brothers will be chosen to the conflicts held within them as the Evil Tahmahnawis' powers grow strong as each rise of the moon draws darknesses evil reign hardened upon us.

I sense the day, given its fasten upon us, shall create havoc and strife, and our lands shall become diseased and lose honor beneath the pass of the Hyas Otelagh.

I, without fault, foresee through these hardships that will soon manifest their compass amongst us, the Mesaschie Tahmahnawis will reenter many souls that have for so many moons strived to dispute their entry within them.

218

And many brother's souls shall be lost to our gather.

So shall they be no more . . .

Many moons have passed beyond the horizons as my people's great chief, and my father, Mokst Tahmahnawis, shared before our peoples of the battles that were once waged between ourselves and our brothers of the south. He spoke of how the Mesaschie Tahamahnawis grew within many of the village's peoples and the Hyas Pishpish grew hungered for their souls.

I knew as I sat before this night's fire and listened to the council of our brothers, that the fight within us shall bring conflict amongst the Spirits that give breath to all life across the kingdoms that we have promised to find honor.

The battle shall begin as told to my brothers by the Kaka's calling of Tenas Pahto, but it is us, all my brothers that have now gathered before our camp that must find fortitude in our beliefs, and through this, our peoples shall prevail safely as the Evil Spirit that breathes disease and pestilence upon our lands shall pass beyond all our villages stake.

Many days had passed as I was turned from my village and followed the trails that led to the Elders that rested high upon the peaks of the Tkope Lemoto.

A long journey that took me far away from my peoples as I found my path crossed by many waters that I had not witnessed to that day. My trail, as the Elders had envisioned me to accept, led me to many sides of Pahto as Lawala Clough stood silent above her lands.

Many Spirits stood far above my travels across the lower lands of my peoples, and from atop the summits that rose above the valley's floors

I was witnessed to Pahto and to the Hyas Tehoma, Mt. Ranier, and as I looked behind to the Lands of the Hyas Wy-East, Mt. Hood, were posed many Brothers and Sisters of the Cascades as their forms were standing proud upon their chairs that rose up overlooking their celebrated lands.

I sensed that all was good within the kingdoms that surrounded our own as their properties were seen thriving, and as I turned from their resonation that was honored unto them by the Hyas Tahmahnawis, I felt sadness quickly drawn within my soul.

As it was my soul that was wrought with despair even as I viewed the beauty of the kingdoms that lay below my rise before the sharpened peaks of the Tkope Lemoto. I knew then what reasoning was so ordered for my presence before the Hyas Elders, and that they would not be chosen for my people's pleasure, but what I am to be lessoned shall take away all that was good from within our purse as we knew it.

"My brothers, as I search the heavens and find that Otelagh has chosen to shed upon us warmth to hold our spirits high before him, I have been chosen to a vision by the Hyas Tamahnawis that spends Otelagh's warmth and may soon lead us away from the gifts that our High Spirit has honored upon us.

Held within the clouds that do not yet pass above us, I sense darkness spelled across all the lands, and as the lands that we are known become unseen before our journeys, our peoples shall be forced to stray from the trails that we are known and be led far distant from those of our villages.

Below all the lands that the Hyas Tahmahnawis rules, and of all the lands of our brothers that we have shared one anothers fires, and of all those peoples that are separate from our lands by the great water, our brothers shall become wanting as life shall change as does the Great River's course upon the challenge of the full, pahtl moon as it lifts from upon the unseen shores that treasure of the sun's rise.

We shall find our waters cast far from the high places that once held the silken robes of our Spirits, and they shall be then chosen to the water's of the setting sun.

As Sun, Otelagh traces across the paths of our heavens there shall be fire and flood, and our lands shall be no more.

Our spirits may become distant from our Great Father's dreams, and our spirit shall be held honorable no more before them if we allow our error before their cast.

We shall be as the striped cat before our Fathers, and they shall flee far from our cast in contempt and regret that we once measured amongst their strides.

Our spirit shall then be wandered amongst the lands of the Great Cat Spirit, Pishpish, and many of our brother's souls shall become separate from our own, and they shall be devoured within its darkened cave.

It will be a lightless day as our peoples have ever shared from the first days we had first chosen these lands amongst the Hyas Tahmahnawis' kingdom, and when the Great Sun again passes over our villages and sweeps across the heavens, he shall see death lain upon his kingdom's floor.

Our souls shall be lain untended and unkept, and he shall know many have fallen far from within his merciful hand.

The great spirits of Pahto and Lawala Clough that rise into the heavens shall soon to that day fall silent and crumble beneath to the valley's floor as the bad spirits that dwell beneath our feet shall tremble with complaint, and they shall be not seen amongst their brothers and sisters once more.

Given this day my brothers, my vision has been told to show that as Sun crosses the trails of his heavens, he shall peer down upon our gather, and it shall be that darkened day that he shall hear our brother's wail, and their voices shall quickly become silent to the winds, and they shall be heard no more.

It has been told that upon the Great Spirits rise from behind the Land's of Wah's highest peak shall be seen a day when Sun peers below his reign and discovers our brother's souls dismembered from his teachings, and from his eyes shall be charged upon them a flood as that once known of Missoula as it too challenged the lands of our brothers from the north to the great waters of the hyas salt chuck.

My brothers, these same tears shall fall from upon his splintered cheeks and cover our lands complete, and with our confusion to the Great Spirit's question, we too may be seen no more.

My brothers, this is the vision that has brought me before your gather here this sad night. It is this one day that shall arise before us without warn from the High Spirit that our peoples shall be in question before him.

We must ask, do we sit silently upon the high peak, telecaset, and allow our brothers to fail before the Great Spirit's passing? Or do we gather upon the highest telecaset and wail before all our brothers of all the kingdoms and warn them of their own absence upon these lands that Sun has promised to claim his own once more?

My brothers, what must we challenge unto our brother's lesson that shall not fail the teachings gifted before us by the Great Spirit?

Where should we, my brothers, point our traces, and amongst what trails shall we journey that shall lead us far from our villages and tend to our brother's before their disorder brings darkness to the heavens above and we fall silent and unseen upon these lands?"

Many seasons had passed from the day I spoke of my vision to my brothers, and our lives were spent under Sun's safe rule as they had been for many turns of his passing above.

Our brothers joined one another's tribe far above the creek of the Eagle for many days as we were gathered to capture many of the Moolack's souls.

Each of our tribes were seen standing upon the rocks that lined the great river as the Hyas Pish were chosen of their run to their village's distant, and pebbled cradle.

Our longhouses drew the smoke for their keep as the Pish were lain before the Hyas Sun to offer thanks before him as we honored the Pish' wanting passage.

Upon our tables were seen a celebration to the spirit's souls that the Hyas Tahmahnawis had treasured unto our gathering.

The Hyas Sun gave us warmth for the berry to ripen upon its vine, and upon our tables were seen a celebration of their gifts before us.

We gave honor to the Hyas Sun as he allowed all our brothers to endure the cold winters that came and passed as we found warmth in the Beaver's, Eena's spirit's pelt.

We were seen to tread lightly across Sun's lands as we found honor in his acceptance of our villages, and through our respect for the lands that he had envisioned for our use, we savored upon all his gifts.

The Great Sun passed overhead and smiled upon us as we offered respect to those gifts that Sun had so honored our peoples.

As we stood amidst the forest's sticks, we listened to the wise words that were spread through their branching arms as they spoke of the same wisdom captured by our fathers, and of their fathers before them of our Great Earth's gifts.

Through our respect, and through our honor of their decree upon Sun's lands, we chose to furrow our canoes from the sticks that lay upon the forest's floor as the winter's breaths drew strong upon their souls and offered their fallen lengths to our use.

And Sun beamed upon us from above, and the forest's sticks grew strong, and their spirits were drawn to the trails that cross the heavens that Sun is traced.

For many seasons our peoples grew passionate beneath Sun's raze, and my vision had not again been spoken.

But as I have journeyed beyond our brother's villages that rest beneath Pahto's kingdom, I have felt the spirits that are held beneath their lands complain as their sticks dance of death as they weaved their forms upon my sides as I had tread upon their claim, and from beneath my stride were seen large furrows widened as the High Spirit's grounds splintered in their chase of my trail. As I returned upon these very trails, and as I was pointed towards our village, these clefts had then doubled as their root had chosen their dislike of my passage across their features.

These lands that I now speak are the high peaks that hold the Tkope Lemoto, and to our peoples these are the elders of all these mountain's Spirits as they had long crossed the horizons of the setting sun and journeyed into the heavens before the days when our peoples first found claim upon these lands that lay beneath their peak's sharpened blades.

The White Goat are the creatured spirits that the High Spirits had chosen to remind those that pass within their properties that they are the most honored upon the grounds of this kingdom.

It is these hallowed grounds that must be held secure as its refuge is where one may gather unto the High Spirit's most advancing call.

The village that I was drawn, and all my brothers that were envisioned to my lesson before them through the Hyas Tahmahnawis' teachings were witnessed to the Menasche Tahmahnawis' turbulent soul upon my return before them, and the Bad Spirit's menacing face was turned towards our brothers, and all that they were known was soon lost as the Bad Spirits that thrived within Pahto's soul gave rise from below the soils of His kingdom.

It was after my last journey north when many of our peoples were joined along the waters of the Wind gathering the red berry and Salmon, and as we stood along the river's banks beneath the cover of the stick's, the leaves that clung to their arms breathed deeply and fell from upon their arms, and a cold wind found its chilling mark upon us.

The soils of the lands that we were gathered began to rumble from afar of our brother's lands, and the swift waters of the Wind began to tumble with great force from within their stream and swelled upon its faltering brace.

Held firmly above our stance to our lands the heaven's breaths held firmly to the wings of Crow as he called out to warn all our brothers that the spirits were unpleased and that we must follow his trail across the heavens if we too were to survive.

The Eagle too cried out as he passed overhead as the Spirit of the White Goat were then firmly chosen to their summons of all the elders to the peoples that had promised of their celebration upon the lands that knelt beneath their chair.

The grounds that surround our peoples along the Wind began to tremble once again, and with a rumble alike the angered voices of the Great Spirits that spread across our lands as their spears are thrust across the sky, there were seen great numbers of deer and elk that fled from within the forest's hidden and safest hides.

High above our gather we had searched unto the heavens towards the Hyas Tahmahnawis' gate, and it was then that we envisioned the Great Sun, Hyas Otelagh hidden, and in pursuit of his moon's descention from the heaven's stellar trails.

All voices of the forest fell mute to our listen as the heaven's light was then challenged from the Hyas Tahmahnawis' trails, and with sorrow held within our hearts, their traces were unfavorably lent unto the shrouding of the evil spirits challenged and blackened draw.

Our fears were pointed to the thoughts of Hyas Otelagh's latent turn, and of the berries that lay unripened upon their vine, and of the Camas that may soon lie weakened and withered to its root.

Upon the paths that the Good Spirit has led us given Otelagh's journeys above his kingdom, we were then witnessed to the heaven's darkened and tragic mast.

We could not see the trail that we were accustomed, and these trails we had often chose to trust our delivery through our lands, but today, this day had turned from light to dark, and we could not find our way across them.

I found fear that our efforts before the Great Spirit were unwelcomed, and that our trails were then surrendered to the Bad Spirits's wanting take.

It was our fates that may have been promised before the Bad Spirits as our faith of the High Spirits were then lain certained to its question as the Great Coyote, Hyas Talupus, soundly mourned across the kingdoms that Sun's rule was treasured.

Our peoples that had gathered along the Great Wind were challenged to climb to higher grounds as the fast waters took captive to all that stood along its fastened point.

Great stones from above the valley's floor rushed before us as they consumed the borders of the Great Forest that once stood proud along the Hyas Wind's greening shores.

Our fears were then pointed to where we must flee to again join the fires of our village, and as we stood in silence and in wait for our Hyas Spirit's guidance, great clouds formed across the valley, and tears burdened with sorrow began to tumble from upon the Hyas Tahmahnawis' cheeks.

Our sights were then lost to our lands that had once lain far below along the Great River as the waters fell tightly bound from the heavens, and the trails to our village were quickly consumed beneath their wake.

And our village was seen no more.

As my brothers and I stood in shock as the waters swiftly covered our village and consumed the lands that surrounded the river's banks, we thought the High Spirits had found difference given our faith unto their lead.

I could not determine where our peoples had turned from the High Spirits wishes as we had promised honor to all that shared the kingdoms that we respectfully paced.

I stood bewildered as did my brothers to the punishment of the Spirit's wrath upon us, and as we joined upon the highest telecaset that gave cover beneath the High Spirit's reign, our wail before them spread throughout the valley and to the lands of the elders distant to our own.

I knew the warning that I had envisioned by the High Spirits many days past had not been chosen by the reasoning of their dislike to our gathering upon these lands.

This I found fear alone in that my peoples may not believe in their guidance through the High Spirit's teachings as I was promised, as now we have nothing, and are to our beginnings once again beneath their storm.

I must fasten my thoughts to my brother's question of our punishment quickly before they turn their thoughts distant from my lead, and I believe that it is not us that is warned by the Spirit's jury upon us as they had not spoke of our harm unto their kingdom's spirits through my vision.

I recount of many seasons when the winter's frozen breaths fell upon us, and that many creatures and many of our own brothers were lost due the storm wrought by the Hyas Tahmahnawis.

Yet we have survived our loss and have furthered our trust to the sanctity of these lands we have been so honored.

I recount to the high waters that had several seasons chosen to rest upon the lands that once stood distinguished high above their channeled reign as the great snows fell from the mountaintops and as Sun warmed the lands suddenly the waters rushed down upon those that they were suddenly drawn.

From these flooded shores we have gathered the Camas root and have trapped the souls of the goose that have given us trade with our brothers from the high desert for the shiny glass that we plane unto our spear's sharpened point, and for the kuitan that we race besides our brothers below Pahto's silenced rule.

I recount to the spirit's breaths that fell whole forests high above the Creek to the Eagle's shores and demanded for them to lie down upon the meadow. Within the borders of these fallen spirits we have culled many moolack and mowitch as they also chose to lie down before us amongst the sticks fallen brothers as they offered their souls upon our tables.

I must recount these memories swiftly before my peoples, and remind them that it may not be to our loss in that the Spirits have chosen to wash away all that we were known.

I must share before them that what is held teemed in the Spirit's storm may cleanse the soils that we were once chosen, and through our loss, we may begin anew upon a highered plain that allows our nearer reach unto the spirit's gated straits.

Our peoples will then again be seen securely marked within Sun's kingdoms.

I ask, "Klakst kunamokst nesika ow winapie miwhit skookum elip okoke Hyas Tahmahnawis' la shase, pe klatawa pe ticky klap kopa yaka elahan kunamokst nika?

"Who among our brothers will stand strong before the Hyas Tahmahnawis' chair and seek his assistance beside me?"

We cowered beneath the stick's cover as the spirit's tears fell hurriedly upon us, and as the Hyas Otelagh finally shone from behind its brother moon, the heavens opened from above us, and mercy was offered unto the kingdom that we stood.

Great walls had formed along the river's course as stones of distant peaks flooded from their perch, and as we climbed upon the soils above the river's trace, and pointed our lead toward Lawala Clough, our question of the spirit's breach was now invoked disheartendly before us.

From the distant heights were gathered great smoke from within Lawala Clough's soul, and it was here that her anger was seen spewed unto the Hyas Otelagh's trails above her.

Great fires were seen falling from upon her flanks as her temper had now grown weary of her unaccompanied stand upon her kingdom as she had once promised her unaccompanied soul to Pahto.

With shame drawn unto her breast by Pahto's deliverance unto his peoples that once lived peacefully beneath his reign with fire and flood, she now drew from within her soul the remainder of her warmth towards him.

Spoiling from upon her silken robe fell fire that drew unto the great sticks as their souls were quickly consumed, and it was there that was delivered her last gasp before all life that once dwelled beneath her witness.

My peoples were then cautioned to Lawala Clough's fearsome quarrel within her, and without thought, were quickly turned to the kingdom of Pahto's welcomed guard.

As Sun has shone his first traces upon our group I have coursed the trail to the river's edge and have peered across the fast waters that shall lead our path before Hyas Pahto and then to the Hyas Lemoto's Kingdom.

Our arrival before the pervading slopes of Pahto shall be sanctioned if the spirits that have once given their choose of our people's demise below their darkened trails allow our safe passage to the far shores where we shall learn of our great leader's charges as they are disbursed upon us.

The river runs fast this day, but as I overlook its pass there are no stick's forms attached to the channels that we must pass, and this has proven that Otelagh has shone above us and has smiled with liking as we have again given thanks to his allowance of our fortune upon his lands, and tears have not again fallen from within his eyes for many days and caused flood to fall upon us.

I have faith that we shall enter within the kingdom that once claimed our brother's lives, and as we have been spelled from our villages, we shall return without loss of our own brother's banding.

In this, we shall set forth before our peoples the trails that our Father's spread before us, these same paths that shall permit life to obtain promise before them.

And the poison of the skugh opoots, rattlesnake, that is swift to its spear within us shall be deprived from its burdening wound . . .

My eyes have peered to the lands where Otelagh rises, and as I was once shown by the Hyas Tahmahnawis' spirit to the signs of approach by the Mesaschie Tahmahnawis' spirit, the stain that is to be attached unto the heaven's trails that foretell of bloodshed and death to follow is not seen to its rise above us.

My faith is again braced, and my hope for peace shall remain strong before all that pass beside me that bring upon its question . . .

And our peoples shall prevail before the face of treachery that the Mesaschie Tahmahnawis depends as it dares entry into our lands,

Our souls shall waiver far from the Evil Spirit's plague . . .

We have afforded our entry into the valley of steam along the lonesome trail that leads to the spirits that dwell beneath Pahto's claim.

Following my lead into Pahto's kingdom are my brothers as we are spent along this path, and as I turn, is shared the triumphant shape of Wy-East as he proudly stands above his lands and guards our return from the counsel set forth by the Kaka's persistent calling from above.

As the stick's outstretched arms raise far into the heaven's trails, they give praise to the Hyas Otelagh's pass with each breath they expel.

It is these same breaths that the stick's share amongst us that we are reclaimed to our vision with renewed strength to our quest . . .

As we strive steadfastly forward, we are yet further impelled by the constant raucous of the Kaka's most fervent screams,

I too cry out,

"My brothers, we must be near!"

Upon the sight of Otelagh's ensuing pass above us, we were seen chosen above the grounds that lay upon the valley of our brother's village.

Our brothers stood unguarded to our approach before them as they too were lain cautioned by Otelagh's shadowed pass above them, and to the remains of the stick's forms that lay flattened along the valley's lower trails.

It could now be heard that through their wail they now lay question before the High Spirit's rage.

High above upon the whetted spearheads of the mountaintops that give sight to Pahto's rule, and to where the Hyas Olallie, Great Huckleberry, grow upon its edge, was heard great thunder as it was here that the Hyas Tahmahnawis' voice was turned towards our gather.

As I now stand upon the telecaset that rises greater than the valley's floor of our brother's village, my spirit strains given my advance upon the lower trail that leads to our brother's village.

I sense hidden by the Spirit's breath's release unto the stick's lowly bow, is now chosen the Mesachie Tahmahnawis that I had been created upon my quest before the Hyas Tkope Lemoto.

Our brother's village, and all that are gathered within are challenged to flee the darkened spirit that has quickly formed before them as the Bad Spirit's heated breaths are promised upon the grounds that they have now chosen to hail.

It is seen that this blacken cloud's shroud has once again formed upon us, and that the chilling breaths of the Spirits have crossed upon our trail alone.

As the grounds beneath us again are challenged by the Hyas Spirit's charge, my brothers of my village stand beside me as we grieve for our brother's souls as the Bad Spirits consume all that is surrendered within their baited and heated wake.

As was witnessed before me in my vision through the presence of the White Goat, our brother's voices were not to be heard again.

And all was silent.

And their village, as it now lies blackened and alone to its boil, shall not be seen again.

And all was lost before us as the darkened cloud that held the Bad Spirits rose up from upon the ground and gave light that our brothers were no more amongst our assembly.

Our spirits were soon lent toward our brother's suffering, and yet we did not understand the reasoning behind the High Spirit's decision that chose for our brother's eviction from the lands that they were chosen.

Our wail before the Hyas Tahmahnawis was spread to all the lands that rose from the valley's floor from where we then stood, and all that we had witnessed was then seen by all our brothers, and our complaint was chosen to the Hyas Spirit's chair that was held secure upon the high peaks of the Tkope Lemoto.

And across the kingdoms that was soon to be heard our wail;

Became suddenly stilled.

And there arose silence unto the Hyas Illahee's beckoning breaths . . .

Chapter 20
Fathered Before the Tkope Lemoto

With our heads held low before the loss of our brothers that have now passed unto the lands of the Lolo our numbers are again pointed to the highest peaks of the Tkope Lemoto.

Our thoughts lie numbed to what we have witnessed as our brothers were imprisoned by the heated breaths that have fallen across the once rich lands that allowed them to reign free from the Bad Spirits.

Our question before the Hyas Spirit of the Tkope Lemoto shall be to what we must do to survive within the kingdoms that the Hyas Tahmahnawis chooses for our hold?

I sense fear within us all as we were well known of our brother's gainful acceptance of the Spirit's trials, and now, even as they held strong to their beliefs, they are not to be seen or heard again.

Each stride that we hesitantly submit towards the high telecaset of the Tkope Lemoto we find our feet to tremble as we become nearer to their foreboding spires that are signaling far distant from Pahto's protective rule.

I sense within our fear we have lost trust to the land's order and of our acceptance before the High Spirits.

It is this fear that I must condemn from our brother's souls before they turn from all that we have been honored, and from all that we have honored of the Spirit's quest for our point.

I must reassure my brothers that we shall rise above all those that have knelt before the smoking grounds that we have found regret, and it shall be turned to my brothers that it is that same regret that we must find strength, and in that strength, our peoples shall be found passionate to our stay.

Many days have passed as we have chosen well of our trail to the high peaks of the Tkope Lemoto.

Our souls have found strength in that the High Spirits have allowed our step to approach their noble seat high above our calling.

I now feel distinguished as my people's leader as the days that have passed behind our strides have promised that our thoughts have chosen to remind of all the lessons we have collected within our souls. In these teachings, the High Spirits have directed us to savor our survival within their kingdoms and all the lands that are spread near and far that we have passed, we have chosen neither failure nor dismissal of our deeds before thr High Spirits.

We shall stand strong and united before the Tkope Lemoto . . .

And we, my brothers all, shall be considered before the Hyas Tahmahnawis' chair.

This night we shall be gathered before the camp's fire and tell of our fortune upon the great river's banks as the Wawa Spirits have flowed untamed by our restraint from the culling of the mightiest of the forest's Stick's Spirits that stand proudly along its shore.

We shall be determined far and wide from our camp's alightened fire, and it shall be heard from above our stay by the Hyas Tahmahnawis that we are juried to Our Great Father's ways.

It is within these very customs that we shall be judged, and if we are found distinct in our endeavors upon their gracioused lands, we shall be led safely from upon their sharpened spires and found nestled beneath the mighty Cascadian peaks once again.

And we shall be seen thriving upon the lands that we have been known to have been claimed once more . . .

As we sat before the fire and watched the moon rise from behind the Tkope Lemoto's muse, the kwel kwel's, owl's call from above us fell mute across the openness of the meadow.

Hushed to the still air that now coursed through our camp, we sat alone, dismissed within our own thoughts to the silence that now fell beside our gathering.

Distracted by the kwel kwel's suddened turn from amongst our gathering signaled forewarning to its own vision above us.

It quickly reminded that it was us that once stood above our brothers and watched in dismay of their dismissal from their lands and from our attachment within their camp.

Yet, it was us that was survived and now find our path beneath our Hyas Father's stance.

The Hyas Otelagh shall rise upon the heaven's trails this next dawn, and we shall then begin our traverse across their slanted slopes, and as we pass before their White Goat's guard, we shall kneel before their most honored chairs.

"My brothers,

To have come this far, to now rise upon the high cliffs of our father's sanctuary. To plead with our Great Spirits for their guidance, you should now be most honored to have taken upon my side to walk amongst the High Spirit's trails as they have claimed this land to be their own.

It is this very land that is guarded by the Tkope Lemoto that leads from the broad shoulders of Tehomas's and Pahto's sheath that we shall find our stature.

Fear not the silence that now falls across the meadow, but be joyous in that we have journeyed far in safety and were safely pointed through the Hyas Spirit's eyes.

The High Spirits shall admire your strength,

And we shall be seen strong before them . . .

Allow within your souls this night the peace that we have known.

Peace from the hostility that we have been witnessed, and through these aversions that have passed our stand above our brother's humiliation, shall ring of our just worth as we have depended our trust unto the High Spirit's judge.

For tomorrow we shall all depend on one another to ascend before the High Spirit's Chair and to kneel before them as one people.

It is that one that we shall be witnessed and judged.

One united within Our Father's ways,

One united through Our Father's long ago journeyed traces.

One united to follow the lessons that Our Fathers shall exhibit before us as we shall lead our brothers from the sharpened teeth of the bad spirit's crave.

Take the kwates, bitterness, of all the yesterdays given our emergence upon this trail that leads before our Father's chair, and turn it into the tsee kahkwa shuga, sweet, taste of the ripened huckleberries that we crave.

When the Hyas Otelagh rises from the east we shall commence upon the trails toward our new beginnings, and through all the teachings that we have been delivered and have alike adjusted, we shall be welcomed before the Hyas Tumtums that we have been told.

Until the rise of the new day and to the new beginnings of our lives my brothers,

To the new day's rise . . ."

As I sit here before the fire, alone, I know tomorrow shall bring harmony unto our voyage through life's journeys.

As we kneel before our Great Father's chair our voices shall be heard throughout the lands that we are known.

Our feats shall be praised as the Lands of Wah offer solitude and safe grotto where many have discovered their likenesses upon the path of righteousness as is spelled before the Walls of Candor at Wahclella.

The Spirits that dwell amongst the falling waters of our lands guide our every decision given our brother's course before all our peoples.

It is our acceptance of the trials that have been shown before us by the Hyas Tumtums that will ascertain honor to our gather before them.

Our dedication to the preservation of life, every blade of grass, every flower, every stick, every wild spirit that thrives amongst our gather, these are the gifts that we have been chosen to preserve for all those that shall follow our strides after we have pretended upon our last breath.

As I peer deeply into the unknownst of this darkened sky above, a lone star traces across the sky. It is this lone star that I sense shall allow our peoples to safely gather within its shadow upon our new village's grounds.

We shall not be delivered distant from one another by our haste in decision to what path we may follow, but in that decision, we shall hold true to our lives, and we shall progress within our people's beliefs as is taught by our Great Fathers beneath the Hyas Otelagh's pass above.

Life must prevail for all humanity to envision Wahclella's most honorable truths.

Our fight shall not be found with another's tribe, but we shall accept our battles to be gained within the salvation and treasuring of life that we have been so honored.

Ikpooie, to shut, my eyes as I lie beneath the stars shall bring enlightenment with the rise and warmth that Otelagh's pass shall soon bare . . .

And all that we know today,

Shall be determined the truth tomorrow . . .

And our peoples shall be found honorable,

And we shall prosper . . .

As the Great Sun rises from behind the screening of the far peaks there is a spoken word from high above our rest,

"Klatowa,

My brothers.

As we have sat upon our chairs high above your peoples for many passes of Otelagh's rule, we have lain witness to your struggles and of your conquests to our wishes.

It has not been solely determined that through your conquests that we have demanded for your ascension before our assembly, but it is of those struggles that you have endured that we have found praise unto your likeness.

The day we first offered our guidance to your sanction within the Lands of Wah was our gift to all your peoples, but it was soon seen that in many of your brother's eyes there was to be seen deceit to our vision, and in that deceit, waste had attached itself deepened to their souls, and they strayed far from our chosen paths as they stood wounded and unknownst to themselves.

We have found that as your brothers had not only failed our teachings, they too had failed you as their thrust before peoples of many different kingdoms were chosen of greed and had brought them notice through their thievery.

As we sat overlooking their dissension from our ways, we grew weary of their likeness as it was cast upon those that knelt beside them solidly in trust.

Your peoples were also trusting of their gather amongst you, and for this, they have now paid their dues solely with what they had left to offer that was theirs alone to control, their own lost souls.

We have chased the bad spirits far from the lands that they were sworn, and now the lands that were once chaste through your brother's disease shall be again free from dishonor and shall not allow humiliation to be afforded your peoples through your own patience and fortitude upon the righteoused trails that we have shared before your strides.

As our tears have swept away all the disease from the lands that your brothers had once fouled, we have come to agree that you may again journey to the Great River's bank and rekindle your souls upon the grounds that you were once known to share.

We ask of you only one matter that you must depend towards your people's survival, and that to be your return upon another's trail, and never shall your entrance again be allowed into the lands that are now lain in blacken ruin from those people's spite given the righteoused path that allows one another's arms to extend allowing to humanities securing hold.

The lands that you had traced to find your stature before us shall now fall from upon the mountain's slope, and where it once stood, shall be held vast wastelands wrought with hot rocks delivered by the baited breaths of the evil spirits that hail from beneath its cover.

It shall also be seen from these lands shall one day rise Pahto's shame before all his brothers and sisters of the Cascades, as he shall wage his most passionate battle against the evil spirits that dwell deep within his soul that thwart his growth before all that surround him.

And Pahto's sharpened peak shall rise no more in stature above you . . .

Chapter 21
Our Faith's Renewal

Each and all of our brothers that had journeyed beside me to the high peaks of the Tkope Lemoto have again joined along the banks of the Great River where once stood our village. All that was once afforded us along the Great River's banks has now been cleansed from the evil that had once been spelled upon these grounds, and we are now safe to begin anew below our Great Father's rule.

We are to believe that as it is our wish to follow within the footsteps of our Great Leaders that we have again been allowed to join our likeness amongst the treasures that we were well known within the properties of the Lands of Wah.

I, with silenced voice and with great measure honored unto the High Spirits share to the heaven's trails as I kneel before the fast waters of the Great River . . .

The Hyas Otelagh rises far above us and sheds warmth and breathes life to all that surrounds our gather, and we are each once again relative to all life's trace upon these grounds.

Through our compassion and approval of one anothers band, we shall all thrive for all the days that shall pass beyond our own.

And life shall be survived . . .

"Mahsie!"

My brothers are once again seen passionate upon the lands that we are again favored to stand as we all join together beneath Sun's pass overhead and build upon the banks what had been taken from what we had thought to be our sanctuary.

And our village shall be whole and favored far from the tears that had fallen heavily across its properties.

We shall offer pish that we have caught from the fast waters to the Hyas Tumtum who we soundly give praise, and we will rekindle our tables with a feast from the souls of all the Hyas Tumtum's gifts that he has offered before us.

And our lives shall begin anew with the first breaths that we have taken beneath the stick's majestic rise far from the water's edge, and all that we have known shall return tenfold before us.

And all that we are gifted shall be presented to those that again accept our stage as they stride forward towards new lands that lie beyond our sights.

And we shall again be one as brothers beneath Hyas Otelagh's rule far above these lands that our hearts are drawn.

Chapter 22
The Bridge of the Gods

The stick's leaves have not yet fallen from their arms, and as the winter's winds have not brought hardship upon us, and the Great River has not yet thundered with much water. We had thought our lives to be safe from the hardships that harden our souls once the Cole Illahee bares its mark within us. But in a swift pass of the Hyas Moon above us the kingdoms have begun to speak amongst themselves and we are now shaken from our longhouse and searching the sky above towards the Hyas Tyhee Saghalie for answers.

What was a silent night with soft breaths of the spirits passing across the lands is not heard or seen again as the spirits have begun to shout between themselves and have chosen to form great smoke to lie closely to the river's fastened course as it falls from far above us.

With anger and vengeance promised of their souls, Wy-East and Pahto have again chosen of their battle.

The brothers of my peoples find their struggle untold as each passing of the day's storm offers spoil to our catch, and as the dark, screening smoke of the two brothers of Hyas Tyhee Saghalie family falls heavily across our lands from above the great valley, we are now sightless to the high peaks of the Cascades most honorable spirits.

With the darkened mast that we are now surrendered first brings heavy till, rains, upon us, and then frozen tears fall heavily upon the lands, and to the peaks of our Fathers above us approach the rains again, and they wash all that was born of the Cole Ilahee's storm far below unto the Great River.

As swiftly as the Great Hawk, Hyas Shakshak, flies across the skies the waters held from above upon the streams of the mighty Cascades tumble to the river and its rise is quick upon us.

Much that we have is soon cast away and lost beneath the swift water, skookum chuck.

Upon each repulsived spell that the bad spirits wish upon us, we find ourselves strained to rebuild our stakes along the river's bank where the mighty Salmon Spirits shall soon fill our nets, and swiftly, the waters rise upon us, and all is again lost beneath the water's fastened race.

As each storm is unleashed upon us and the sky remains dark and the breaths of the Chinook remain frozen and fall deep and hardened beneath our strides we find ourselves to question why before the merciless hand of the high spirits that had once wished us favor, and as they prey on our faith before them we are now led to our question.

As we have awaited the waters to retreat, we had not lost honor beneath the Hyas Tumtum's vision, and it was then that our nets are again filled for many days, and our catch was plenty.

We have seen when the Salmon Spirits choose to fill the waters of the Great River as the forests above the river's shores would again lay claim to the leave's fall, and they too would return tenfold before us.

Upon the Great Sun's rise high above us, and rising from the depths of the great river from their return of distant waters, great numbers of Salmon would pass below our feet, and upon the lands shall again soon be offered Camas and berry to settle upon our tables.

To all that we have been offered, we ask not for more . . .

High above our village that we had joined to the grounds at the foot of the Big Rock was heard deep thunder echoing across all the valleys surrounding us.

Many of our brothers were fishing from the high rocks from the point of the land that stretches far into the Great River, and as the ground began to shake and the voice of the spirits was loudly cast upon us, was then seen smoke lifting far into the heavens from the Spirit's highest place.

We envisioned a large herd of Elk had begun to choose their escape towards the lower valleys from the next storm's approach, but as the sound grew faint and the cloud did not approach towards us, we knew the Spirits of Table Mountain, Tahmahnawis La Tahb Stone Illahee, were suddenly angered by the spirits of the rock that were then falling from upon their divided shoulders that lay sullenly untied from their union, and as rebels to their cause before their brothers above the Hyas Columbia, they were assured to be cast out from their tribe.

We are understanding as it was the spirits of the mountain that had cast down their fallen brothers as they were often seen standing weak upon their flanks as each spring their souls cried out for mercy.

We have crossed over these lands many times and have followed the deer and elk's trails across the fallen shoulders of the great mountain as we surrendered our souls before the Kingdom's of Lawala Clough and of Pahto, and it was then as we rose up before the broken lands that the most humbled of the mountain's spirits had been seen falling in disgrace beneath to the valley's troubled floor.

Their souls were lost to all that would climb upon the mountain from that day's passing of the Hyas Tyhee Saghalie, and their rank upon the great telecaset, hilltop, would be seen no more.

The air grew silent as we awaited the return of the thunder from above, but as the light began to fall from the heavens and find their souls kindled into the far lands of our brothers, we then chose our return to the longhouses of our village.

As the darkness of night settled, and before the black bear begin to stalk its next prey we placed the pish's spirits before our Great Spirit upon their shelf as they lie drying before the return of the White Swans, Tkope Kahloke, as their numbers would soon reappear above us and alarm us of winter's return as it shall settle upon us without further sign.

As the leaves have fallen from the stick's arms and the great winds have now begun to cross the lands of our Hyas Kingdom we have taken shelter from their storm.

High up upon the cliffs edge we have seen the white beard of winter fall upon their faces, and as the winter spirit's breathes heavily upon us, we hear the voices of the rock's spirits that are held high above our village cry out as they too have fallen victim to its mighty powers.

As Sun has passed across the heavens for many days unseen, the spirits held within Pahto and Wy-East has begun to awaken once again as their thunder is chosen to echo across all the lands, and are quickly pointed towards one another's kingdoms in their disgust for one another's fiery temper.

The ground has shook each day that they have shared angry words across to one another, and as they wish to find fight with one another and not settle their dispute peacefully, they each attempt to lay claim to the bountiful lands of the Wisscopam.

We have yet to see if they have begun to build fires and send smoke unto all their brothers and sisters of the Cascades, but we know our wait is not long as they both beat upon their drums repeatedly and with greater force and intent.

With great fury, words are spread of their fight amongst our peoples. Many brothers have begun to find their claim within our village and far from the treasured lands below Pahto.

All the animal spirits of the forest that had found safety once again below Pahto have also given chase to the lands of Lawala Clough and of Tehoma, and as we stand looking far to the north and south towards the Tyhee Saghalie's sons, many Mowitch and Moolack draw amongst us for safety. The Hyas Klale Lolo also has found shelter near us, and far above our village we hear the cry of the Pishpish's gravest spirit.

All the animals of the Hyas Sticks have joined amongst us, each sharing amongst their own and fearing not of the other.

We do not know what is to become of the fight above us, but we have taken notice that the Hyas Spirits are now maddened beyond retreat, and we too must find shelter quickly from their storm upon us.

As each shout from the two brothers are cast across to one another the message that is sent between them creates panic within the forest, and the sticks that surround our village sway with their own passion, just as do the tall gray Kalakala with red hairs crowned upon their heads dance before their own tribe's welcomed gathering.

Many sticks begin to crack and fall deafeningly upon the hardened ground from their place as their spiritless souls surrender themselves from the trails that once led our eyes unto the heavens.

Each tree falls disgraced in different paths from one another as they are alike a tribe lost from one another.

As they have chosen not to stand proud and spread their magnificent arms towards the avenues of the heavens where Sun had first lent them, their souls are now devoured by the Mesahchie Tahmahnawis' hunger, as it has now taken upon their souls and forced their kneel before his pitiful table where lies hidden only hate and disorder by his ruse.

It saddens us as we know that these sticks shall not be seen standing in great strength as they had once been seen to stand proudly before us as we knew them, and their souls are forever lost to those peoples that one day will pass across these lands from this day forward.

The great Earth trembles as each brother holding of the Great Spirit becomes angrier with their shouted turn towards one another, and as their roar is heard and their intent felt deep within all our brother's souls throughout the kingdoms of the Cascades, it too promises fear to invest sadly within the bird's cautioned flight.

Great numbers of Kalakala fly from their villages above us as they too are suddenly unsettled to their perch upon the sticks. With swift wings they now follow the river's turn and point to the waters of the settting sun and will soon find their homes upon a distant land unseen and far from our own.

And they too are soon to be lost to this land's treasured keep until the brothers return to their peaceful closure of their battle.

As we sit high up upon the mountain top and lay caution to the river below us, we watch the water's dance within their channel. With each maddened shout of the brothers, and with each shake of the land, the waters of our lands are too destined to flee from their brace as they choose to build upon their dam and hold threatening above our village, and upon the change of a single breath that we take they suddenly turn to flood and take upon their exit and reach out for new lands to give birth to life along their visceral trails.

Our fears are created now from the unknownst of all that is cast upon us as Wy-East's and Pahto's voices are heard above the roars of the water's lap against the rock that borders their swift fall to the Great Waters below. Hot ash falls before our feet and once again spears are cast far into the heavens above them.

We question to the spirits and of their anger towards us and of our lands as they fight between one another for new lands that lie distant from those that were once gifted upon us beneath their reign.

We receive no answer from above, and our cries fall silent upon the drifting winds that smell of danger and offer pretense of our own destinies.

We are tied to these lands by the order of the Hyas Tyee Saghalie, and we must find our stay upon them or we may not find new lands where we shall discover our survival by our High Spirit's order.

I call to my brothers and ask for them to sit before the fire and speak of their thoughts to this crazed lash by our spirits upon us.

My own thoughts are as questioned as to the trees sway upon these grounds, but through my lessons before Wah's Spirits, I have faith that this will pass and that we shall survive and confess before those that appear before us that we are the chosen peoples to this land, and that it is our order from the Hyas Chief that they must also trek in reverance across our trails upon his lands of this kingdom, and to all those lands that they may pass upon that they have not yet to reach.

As the sun has again shone its last rays that offers warmth upon us, it has begun to settle beyond our lands, and now the brothers have settled upon their disagreement, and the ground dances no more.

Our call unto to the Hyas Spirit for calm to return upon our gathering has been accepted, and all our peoples can now find rest for the night without fear as darkness begins to fall between the trees that still stand amongst us.

"My brothers, we are yet welcomed to our stay within the Lands of Wah. Fear not the sway of the Mesachie Tahmahnawis as it has found its bond upon the grounds around our gather and has now lost strength as the brothers have too chosen to dismiss their feud.

We must find strength in our faith in that the bad spirit will not choose of our souls through the darkened night if the brothers awake and breath fire from their bellies and throw spears across the lands of their kingdoms."

I find little rest myself as I awake throughout the night as my soul is still troubled as I sense the brothers of Tyhee Saghalie are gaining strength and threatening war between one another. I know as the trees have fallen so near our camp that we must be quick upon our feet and dismiss ourselves if their war pretends upon these grounds and quickly swarms upon us and finds us all encircled by their trap.

I find that the brothers have not heard from Otelagh as his voice has yet lain silent as he passed overhead as they quarreled.

I do find faith in that Pahto has stood in silence and in repose for many moons, and that he has sworn to never find fault with Wy-East again as Wy-East gave to him many of the animals and peoples that he made promise of their keep below his throne high up upon his silken robe.

Possibly this is only a quarrel between the two brothers that will once again find peace and calm to the lands and the earth shall again fall silent beneath their deceptived play.

There is always hope and faith that shall keep our thoughts chosen to our forefather's journeys as they too stood upon the two brother's kingdoms as both Pahto and Wy-East found battle between themselves, and our forefathers too survived to speak of their honorable stay before all the brothers that were swayed before them.

"Let them not pretend upon their promise and display their guise before us all!"

We must all have faith in our Hyas Tahmahnawis as he shares wealth and knowledge through his teachings if we walk amongst his strides within his lands. The same lessons that all our fathers and their fathers before them have been led before us, and in their passing of these same lessons, we are survived to teach those of yet to follow of our own.

Our lives were uninterrupted for many days and when the fast waters ceased their boil we gathered upon the high rocks and gathered the great salmon within our nets as they attempted to pass on their journey home.

Many days the Hyas Otelagh passed overhead, and we gave thanks as the ground did not tremble with fear towards Pahto's and Wy-East's further fume. But as the heavens above them cleared from the smoke that had settled upon their crowns we looked to both brothers, and sadly, their crests were now ablaze with flames, and their white robes were no more upon them.

As the air was silent from the high peaks, we knew that their breaths were now labored. Yet, we saw white smoke lifting unto the heavens as Sun passed overhead from within the brother's bellies, and it was clear that peace had not yet touched their souls.

This gave us cause to be alarmed of their refusal to find peace within their caustic souls.

It is a question of how far a crow flies upon a given day before they would find battle across their lands once more.

Again, we may find ourselves fleeing the refuge of our village until the storm of their battle is fraught with complaint by the Hyas Saghalie Tyee.

"May it be soon quelled!

May It Be Soon Quelled!

May their silence bring peace and harmony amongst us all that pretend these kingdoms are ours alone, and may the crow fly to the sticks nearest lodge, as they are both gathered safely beneath Multnomah's tower."

We have gathered to the fire of our camp this eve and we each have chosen to reach upon the mountain's tower above the Hyas River before tomorrow's light and our hunt for the deer and elk to replenish our stock. We must be prepared to last before the brother's fight if it is again to rise above the Illahee's of Wah, and it is certain if they choose to continue that they shall direct their spells upon one another's kingdoms, until their fight for the lands of the high grounds of the Wisscopan shall be determined solely by their wasteful poach.

We have risen from our beds as the Hyas Coyote calls upon the falling of the moon that will soon welcome Sun to soar above us and cast warmth to our souls, and we climb higher towards the great peaks above.

As we near the final ridge of the peak where we have seen trace of the deer and elk we chance to cross a land that is now opened to its bowels before us. The bad spirits have now set themesleves free upon us, and as we all gather and stare desperately at the cadence of the bad spirits march before us, we agree that we must not climb higher upon the bad spirits grounds and must swiftly find our trail towards the sea before their evil spirits return and lay claim to our unguided souls as we fall into the darkened dens where they await.

As we turn from these haunting lands that breath destruction and death to those that enter their domain, we can now hear loud hissing from within the great rocks that cling to their unknowing host, alike that of the mighty Pishpish when she is cornered by our tracking to the capture of her crazed soul.

With each stride that we push forward in retreat the stones are strongly counseling of their release of the waters that have been held within them.

What we had first heard rising as hisses and moans from within the chasm's depths have now turned to screams, such as those heard from the Hyas Pishpish before its strike upon our brother's backs so long ago.

Our trail is quickly set distant from the bad spirits lodges, and yet the ground is heard crying out in pain, and dirt and smoke arises from within its broken spine as far as we can see into the heavens.

Great thunder has begun to shake all the lands around us, and heavy smoke has covered the peaks where we had last claimed our rise upon them.

We must turn away and grant the bad spirits their quarry, and let our souls be freed from their complaint as we promise our retreat before them.

With fast feet we follow the trails of the mowitch and moolack that lead below to the Great River, and as we near its shores the mighty sticks again dance to their own drum and sway unto their spirit's last gasping breaths.

Our feet are shaken from our hold upon the grounds as are the trees that now dance before us. Our strengths must be in our belief in the Hyas Tahmahnawis teachings as he has stated unto us that if we are to be accepting of his way that our peoples must find their survival beside all the animals and plants of their Illahee for all the suns and moons to pass.

As we have fallen upon the frenzied grounds and have no support to lean, I fear our souls may be lent to the bad spirits if they are to become suggestived to our fear of their poach.

My thoughts are now directed beyond those lands that we had found our acclaim upon, as great thunder is cast upon us as coarse as those spirits that once screamed from upon the highest telacasit as their brother's long spears passed through the heaven's trails and found their deathly and fiery strike into each of their lands.

Great clouds begin to cover the lands with sand and rock, and from the rocks that were once held high above the plain where they have fallen, flows rivers of mud and water as they have released the imprisoned souls that had long been held well hidden within them.

From far away above the shores of the river where our village now stands we can hear that great walls are falling from upon the mountain's edge.

Each with great force, and cries from the mighty stick's souls can be heard as they too are surrendered from their hold upon the Great Earth's floor.

As each rumble from above by the spirits fell upon our ears we found fear in that great walls of water and mud followed their course towards us, and our escape was then quickly chosen to be far from along the Great River's banks.

The waters have become white with rage, and their spirits too have rose high upon the shelf of the river as they pass swiftly beside us.

We have no escape!

Our canoes are lashed high above the raging waters, and it is here that we must build fires and sit to keep warm as the darkened skies have stolen the heat of day.

Our faith is again tested by the Great Sun Spirit's dismissal above us as the heavens are darkened to the light's ray, and day is alike the deathly mark left by the bad spirit's daunting hunt for our souls at night.

The voices of the heavens are heavy upon us as great lances are again cast across them, and we hear screams for forgiveness from upon the lands that the brother's spears have chosen to punish.

As my people and I sit before the fire of our camp I sense that we are in loss in that our passage unto the Great Heavens above has been countered by the Mesachie Tahmahnawis, and that all that we have campaigned to protect before all our brothers of these lands and of the kingdoms that surround us is certainly soon to be lost.

High up, distant to our camp, a woman begins to wail unto the angered skies.

With each thundered clasp above us her shout is chosen to the Hyas Coyote's yelp, and she too has become lost to our vision. Her faith flies swiftly from her soul as does the soul of the pish that is captured within the talons of the mighty Eagle as its fight to return home is sadly taken from it.

We now plead unto the heavens to the Hyas Kloshe Tumtum Tahmahnawis beside her to allow her to find her faith once again as we too are heard of our shout before the Hyas Tyhee Tahmahnawis,

"ÒIskum nesika kahkwa nesika skookum kopa wepht mitwhit kwelth elip mika.",

"Save us so we can again stand proud before you, and take not our stake from within your treasured lands as we follow upon your Spirited trails."

As many days passed the ground is again settled under our feet, and the darkened clouds that had spread gloom and cold has begun to lift from upon the floor of the valley and offers light and warmth upon us once again.

Hope that life will again be as it once was has returned and has given us renewed strength.

We had dared to journey to the land where the thunder rose upon us, and as the air is again still we have chosen to find our trails along the great river to where we can look far up into the lands that gave chase to our souls.

As we find our claim along the banks of the river we discover there is little water fleeing to the sea, and is thick and dark alike the lowlands below Multnomah's guard given the return of the stick's leaves of spring.

Silence lay ahead as we pass beyond where our village once stood. A silence as though all that was is now dead. There are no songs spilled upon our ears by the birds fastened to the Chinook.

All that was alive with life has now vanished beneath the storm wrought by the bad spirits as mountains of rock and mud, and fallen forests lie before us as far as we can see to the lands of the rising sun. What was once green with life has now been taken by the Mesahchie Tahmahnawis and turned to mud, and the fallen spirits of the sticks that once clung tightly to the mountain's prolific peaks lie helpless and unmoving.

With saddened eyes we bow in shame before Otelagh as he returns to the heavens above us.

All that was treasured to our lives is now lost to us forever.

As we climb upon the highest peak of this new land, and crest its tower we are crippled as we look across where once flowed the great river.

"What has become of our treasured lands," we ask?

"Where have all our brothers and sisters gone whose lodges once stood proudly beneath us?

What of the salmon that found this home upon their return from the Hyas Salt Chuck?"

All that we knew is now lost before our saddened eyes!

What we do not understand creates panic and fear within us, and our faith flies quickly from our souls as we lay witness to the devastation beneath!

I fear the Hyas Chackchack shall journey unto anothers land, and all that we have given to these lands shall be quickly forgotten as what we had fought to preserve has now been taken from us.

And our visage to these lands shall not be seen nor heard again amongst these lands that we have yearned to bring ourselves honor before the gates of the Hyas Tumtum!

I ask; "Where are we to go if not here in these lands that we have been so honored?"

Chapter 23

Spring Salmon Festival
Tenus Waum Illahee Pish
Hiyu Muckamuck

Many long days and nights had passed as we again found favor
beneath Otelagh's pass, and as the Cole Illahee, winter, was
separated from its storm upon us, Sun rose far into our heavens and
shone brightly across the tiicham, lands.

The sticks were thick with new leaves fastened to their branch and
they sang pleasingly unto the warm breezes that now warmed their
souls. The latit, wildflowers, also took rise from the soils where they
were lain and stood tall from upon them as their sweet scent swept
across our lands.

Tl'alk, deer and elk were seen playing in the meadows as their
newborn breathed new life unto their gathering herd, and all life as
we know it was seen to be happy to be adjoining one another again
across our kingdom.

Our peoples were pleased that wuuxam, spring, was upon us, and all
the women of the villages and tribes that joined in this pawanikt,
ceremony, began to make ready the sacred grounds where we all offer
thanks to Hyas Sun for all the gifts that he has honored us upon the
kingdoms of Wy-East, Pahto, Lawala Clough, to the kingdom where
Sun first rises high into the heavens, the Oluk Snake, and of all the
lands beyond our vision's reach.

Our brothers of the Wayampam, Celilo, Mamachatpam, Yakama, the Paiute, and the Nez Perz that ride far upon their maamin kusi, appaloosa horse, the Amatalamlama, Umatilla, and the Xwalxwwaypam, Klickitat, all join alongside the Great River and spread across its waters ik'walxisha, fish nets to capture the spirits of the nusux, Chinook Salmon that have now returned to their ayaash, spawning grounds.

The Multnomah and the Cathlamet were the last to arrive before our gathering, and from within their purse they place the souls of Akak, Canada Goose, and the xatxat, duck, upon the tkwatatpama, table to give thanks for what they too have been honored.

I too had taken my place upon the edge of the river's bank and gave thanks to Hyas Otelagh as the Hyas Pish's souls passed abundantly beneath me through the wanawish, swift water's.

Each of our brother's villages have carried their ceremonial kiwkiwlaas, drums, and have disbursed them to each corner of the village, and as they have completed placing them they begin to announce through the rhythym of their beat that our gathering has begun and that our spirits are viable and strong beneath Sun's approving pass overhead.

As the Hyas moon rises unto the darkness of night our village stirs with excitement, as the women dance before the fires of our camp and announce through their passionate step their many thanks to the High Spirit for all that they have gathered, and all the young women too dance as they announce through their own passionate steps that their eyes and hearts have yet to be set toward a piitl'iyawila, warrior's counsel of their choice.

As Sun crosses overhead the second day, each tribe of our large village points to their best hunter and we all gather our twinpaash, bows, and set forth to match our skill upon the targets that stand distant from our camp.

As I am Nenamooks, Land Otter, and the son of Mokst

Tahmahnawis, Two Spirits, I too have joined in the festivities of this match.

Throughout the day's light as we continued to match our skills against one another, our numbers began to thin, and only the best hunters still stood before their targets. We each offer gifts of arrows and chukwsh, black glass, to shape our arrow's points, and with furs and hides we reward those that do not miss their mark.

As sts'at, night, falls silently across the kingdom of Wah, and the call of the coyote spills across the valleys where we are gathered, we applaud all those left standing and wish for each of them to return upon first light of the next pass of Sun and take their place before their targets until only one still stands amongst all his brothers.

I have joined these matches many times, and only once was I the victor, and to that day my father was as proud as I given my rise before all my brothers and before all the best hunters of the villages that have joined the Waum Illahee Pish Muckamuck, Spring Salmon Festival.

As Sun favors our council and passes quietly overhead upon the third day, all our tribes are to gather before the camp's large fire at the center of our camp. Young and old alike would then join together and waashat, worship to the rhythym of the Great Drums as their souls rise up to touch the heavens and offer thanks to the Hyas Tahmahnawis, Great Spirit.

As I sit before the fire my soul is drawn by the song of the drum's pulse, and my eyes are quickly turned to a young and beautiful ayat, woman, that has travelled far from where the Yakama are gathered upon their kingdom north of the Great River, and below the Hyas Spirit of Pahto.

I have asked to what her name would be and am told that it is as is the first flower to rise up from the winter's snow in the spring, for she is called Pupseela.

As Pupseela stood and took her place upon her earthen stage she began to dance to the song of the Spilyay, Coyote's Spirit, and as she danced to each edge of the stage she began to spread her own beautiful petals before our wanting eyes.

I could not find myself to look away from her beauty, and I took notice that her feet moved silently and with grace as does the feet of the xwayawi, mountain lion, as it races through the lawiishkishits, shadows, of our kingdom.

Her shimx, dress, was beautiful as it was gathered with bright k'pitlkma, beads, and it was combed with strips of tl'alk apax, deer skin, that were drawn further from the fringes of her dress and hung appealingly along her slender arms.

I knew as I witnessed the dance that Pupseela had chose to share before us all that she had also chosen to share her timnanaxt, story, through the markings of her chalutimash, design.

Upon her feet were lk'am, moccasins, created with the finest of suede and were covered with bright tsimtsim, beads, and from her lulukashs, breasts, hung beautiful beads that she had fashioned to further spell us all to her beauty.

A waxwintash, basket, draped from her k'wi, waist, and told of her name, and through its colorful weave it was easily seen that her promise to her peoples would bring honor and respect unto her ttawaxt, families, name.

I stood in awe to her every step across her stage, and as she turned slowly towards me with the rate of the kiwkiwlaas', drum's cadence, her spirit lingered before me though she had again turned to step to the distant edge of the ring in her k'upip, circle dance.

The light of the ilkwsh, fire's, flame spilled softly upon her long tutaniik, hair, that pleased me as it flowed from upon her k'amkaas, shoulders, and the fire's flame added color to her most beautiful and mysterious achaash, eyes, as she turned and smiled in my direction.

I knew at that moment, though it seemed to never pass, that my eyes and heart were then hers if she were to accept.

Her beauty and grace had enveloped my heart and had easily stolen my soul, and I was as lost to myself by her as I was lost to the Hyas Spirit's lead as I had been spelled absent before them upon the day that the Smoke Spirits arose before me and I was blind to all that lay alongside my feet.

My heart was not mine again, and as I watched Pupseela the call of the huyanikt, love song, of the Coyote Spirit rose up from the Valley of the Eagle where we were gathered just as Pupseela passed beside me, and I knew that she would be to me just as the Coyote's soulmate was to her.

My kwyamtimt, promise to Pupseela would be that I would not be known as the lost coyote's soulmate as she cried to the essence of the moon each night for his return beside her, but as I am now drawn towards Pupseela's inspiring step and most passionate heart, we would be drawn tight unto one another's arms each night.

Our promise to one another would be to share our atawit, love, for all the tminwa, days and nights, that we would be gifted to share together upon our tiicham, land, and that a son would soon arrive and be promised by my lead to our Father's way until his own passage before the Hyas Spirits appeared before our opened door.

Pupseela and I have stood proudly together in all that we have shared, and I am today as I was that night to the light of our own fire's first flame.

Taken of my timna, heart, by the delicacy of her beauty, and stolen of my wak'ishwit, soul, by her poised and appointed step . . .

Chapter 24

When Spirits Once Ran Free

Many suns have passed since my grandfather sat beside me at our campfire and led me through the days when many rivers coursed through our lands without pause. He told me of awakening in the morning before the great sun rose from upon the furthest horizon, and as it first shared its warmth upon the shores of the great river, it was here that he said he found himself many times listening to the water's lap against the rocks that were cast far from the north by the Great Spirit, Missoula.

My grandfather told me of the salmon spirits owning to Goddess Metlako, and of their leap far into the sky as they found great favor in that the waters ran strong beneath them, and this he told was to allow their spirits to inspire to their young to return one day from their life's journey to the great water's of the setting sun and give life so they too would be survived for all the days to pass.

My grandfather sat beside me many nights as the moon glimmered upon the grounds that we shared as he told me of stories such as these of our people's gifted existence within the Lands of Wah.

My grandfather was a great man who's wisdom was never questioned by our peoples as he spoke of the Great Earth, and of the trials that soon would be placed before us.

He spoke of visions that appeared before his eyes to many storms that would soon arise from beyond the horizons of our lives due to mankind's greed and convictions between wealth and preservation, and this vision too has now arose upon us and has shone its repulsive face above the horizon given this very morning's, light's, darkened screen.

Sadly, as had my grandfather once seen, I now give witness to the Great Sun Spirit as it rises from beyond the tainted stains that are attached to the Hyas Tumtum's village.

Today, as I walk along the shoreline of this great river, I see the pish spirits that were once seen pure and free are now fouled as their souls have been held captive and imprisoned behind the tribes of broken stones that rise far from upon the water's plane.

Today, as I am not able to witness to the great salmon's leap toward the trails of the heavens from within the water's crippled stream, I know of the salmon's solitary trap.

The fish spirits that pass below me as I stand upon the shore of this mighty water share the story of their soul's distress and how they have lost their course upon the great river's channel, and how they are now destined to drift in silence toward the darkened depths well hidden by the bad spirit of the salt chuck.

My grandfather told me of the days when he journeyed with his father through the great mountains and valleys that rise along the Great River that was formed by Wy-East's and Pahto's shame, and how they stood beneath magnificent tumwaters, and these water's spirits then calmed their souls as it fell treasured before their feet.

As I also stand beneath these tumwaters today, the Spirits that the Land's of Wah are treasured allow me to peer deeply into the dancing colors held within their teardrops that surrounds me before they fall silently at my feet.

As I enter through the passageway that these colors lead my eyes to stray, I am greatly saddened to witness that the lands and rivers that our peoples had once protected through our respect for the gifts that the High Spirit had chosen for our share, may soon disappear beneath the rising storms wrought by our own undaunted haste.

As the future of our peoples pass nearer to this shameful day through the vision wrought by the High Spirit's wish, I fear that our peoples will not again see these gifts awarded before us!

My vision leads me to the sight of our peoples that shall become lost and forever wandered upon the sand's of the Great Desert! The same desert that is to rise from upon the burnt soils that our lands shall then offer for our survival.

I fear that our peoples shall then become challenged without support from the Hyas Tumtum of our Illahee, and we shall not survive our error!

My grandfather once shared with me the story of seeds that were cast upon our lands by the heaven's breaths, and they were watered by the tears shed by the Great Earth Spirit as he was pleased, and he gave life to the trees that stand proudly amongst our forests.

As I now stand beneath the protection of these tree's surviving brothers, the tears that should now trace steadily upon their sainted root fall silently from upon the arid trails splintered upon the High Spirit's cheeks.

I have seen tall wind catchers strewn across our lands as if they were now graveyards placed upon our lands, and from their sharpened blades they steal the breaths from the winds of the Hyas Chinook. As we sit quietly upon the highest telecasit and peer across the plains and over the mountain's tops, from the sharpened blades of these

276

same wind catchers that are now littered across all our lands, the beautiful birds that had once fed upon the grasshopper and sang pleasingly of their own gifts that Otelagh wished for them now lie without spirit and song.

Their freedom is too taken from beneath their windless and feathered wing and their souls lost forever as they are drawn into the Mesachie Tahmahnawis' most daunting blades well hidden within their sheaths.

They too shall not be seen again . . .

I search unto the heavens for an answer from our High Spirit, and as I plead before him to spare our peoples from the loss of his gifts that are treasured to these soils, I find, held taut to the trails that the sun now traces, and tainted far across the kingdom of the heavens, a red hue stained upon it as if death had bled across its horizons. The same color as was once seen to be our own brother's blood as they had lain untended and stained upon the bad spirit's grounds, as they too once fled the wisdom cast by the Good Spirit to grasp upon the relevance of our faith before him.

This quest, as was my grandfathers and fathers before me, demands my wail before the Hyas Tumtum as I ponder upon our people's allowances once we have allowed the final battle to its promise of our defeat to be cast upon us.

I must question before the people's of this Illahee of our survival without the gift of Moolock, and Mowitch, and the Hyas Chakckak?

I ask, "What of the cry of the Coyote, and what of the song of the whale?"

What must we, as peoples of this Hyas Illahee concede to again allow all the Illahee's spirits to once again be set free?

Chapter 25

My Totem Draws Breath Unto Life

I set upon a journey one day as the sun rose above the crowns of the tall Firs and Cedars that lined the bank of the great waters flowing freely below our village. I was selected to learn of my unique status amongst all the animals and birds, all the insects and snakes, the butterflies and the bees. I was not only to learn of whom I am, but of whom I am through all the living creatures, large and small. All living animals and plants offer support and guide my every step each day as I walk across their grounds, beneath their skies, and within their fast waters, as I was soon to learn.

These were the days that I journeyed from upon the trails of my brothers that Hyas Otelagh has discovered their choices now to be unwise and to bring instability before all that they speak.

These were the days that Otelagh chose to distance me from where I had allowed my spirit to lead, and to take me safely from deep within the darkened hides of the Mesachie Tahmahnawis' tomb where life passes beneath death's darkened mask.

These were the days that I discovered myself, as my soul had been absent from the Hyas Otelagh's path because my feet had yet to follow closely to his trail.

My ears had yet to hear his call, and my fingers had yet to touch the places directed by his long arms.

These were the days I was led by Hyas Otelagh's appointed teachers to expel from my soul my carelessness and lead me once again to breath the unspoiled air that life was promised to thrive.

These were the days I toured through all that Otelagh had passed, through light and darkness, through life and death.

Upon each trail that our high spirits hold within their purse, I was led.

As I stepped upon the river's bank I heard a cry descending from the sky above me, and as I peered to the Hyus Tumtum's lodge a beautiful Osprey soared high upon the thermals that are raised distant from the fast waters as it cried out for the mighty salmon to rise from beneath the water's depths.

Suddenly it dove beneath the water's plane and quickly rose up with great strength as it clasped in its sharpened talons a great salmon.

It is told that when we search our souls and the Osprey appears before us as it dives beneath these same waters and grasps tightly to the spirit of the fish, this is the time that we need to search our souls and awaken our senses as we shall soon discover change to appear in our lives, and through this vision we will certainly be set forth to a better understanding and strengthen our commitment to what Otelagh's lessons teach.

I followed this great fisher as he flew across the waters, and he was soon to perch upon a large branch extended by my old friend, Great Cedar.

I had longed to return beneath Great Cedar's rise and share of our stories, and as I stood witnessing to this Osprey's perch my feet were quick to gather the path beneath them.

Silently I approached Great Cedar to not frighten the Osprey, and as I neared Great Cedar's welcoming arms above me, I found myself to rest beneath his tower and be taken by his softened bark's heavy and sweet scent once again.

Great Cedar welcomed me as we were old friends that had not passed alongside one another for many moons, and as I sat and listened to his stories he began to explain that soon there would be a Kokostick that would direct me upon the trail that I was to follow given his poll upon Great Cedar's trunk.

As Great Cedar and I shared our stories once more, along with old and new visions we had witnessed since the day of our last visit beside one another, the Kokostick settled below the Osprey and began to tap out the map that I was to follow in my travels beside the great river. Upon every step and turn chosen by Otelagh, his rhythmical poll rose up upon the winds of the Chinook and were spread downriver to those that I would soon pass.

As I sat beneath Great Cedar and listened to my journey I began to question why I was to venture far from my village alone without further word to my village of my surrender to our camp's fires, or to when I would return before them again?

With thanks to Great Cedar for his welcoming host I knew it was time for me to rise and follow the trails that Otelagh had told Kokostick to share with me, and with a promise to return beneath Great Cedar's welcoming branch, I swore.

Though I silently questioned Otelagh's upcoming lesson, my feet willingly traced the very grounds that he chose for my entrance before the watery hides that I was soon to be lent.

The light shared by Otelagh passed quickly overhead as I came upon many brothers of our nation that too found their villages staked upon the river's bank. As I entered into their village an elder stepped before me and told that he too knew of my travels, and that if I were to follow beneath Otelagh's trail amongst the heavens, I would soon understand the purpose for my journey.

Each elder that stepped before me that day explained that my journey should be understood to be alike the return of the Salmon Spirits in our rivers and streams.

Each elder chose to share that even though my journey shall take me far from my village, that my return shall be rewarded ten fold, and all that I know today would be changed, and all that changes will find its reward upon all our tables with restored faith and anewed beginnings.

This, the elders shared, shall take us far into the suns and moons that will bring prosperity given Otelagh's pass overhead.

As I listened to each of their stories I hear the same words spoken, the same lessons shared. Though each of the elders shares their stories in a different tone, they each spell upon me the same understanding and ending to my journey that lies ahead.

With each of their stories I begin to question if I am to be alike the Salmon upon my return and take on the shape of the Hyas Pish?

As the heavens begin to turn from light to darkness, I have reached the edge of the forest where I am soon to enter upon the return of Otelagh.

I have found a soft bed of boughs lying beneath the towering arms of another Cedar, and it is here that I gather to their limb and raise their branches from the ground where they had come to rest.

It is at this forest's entrance that I have made camp and await the arrival of Otelagh's warming rays above me. I shall then enter into the beginning of my quest as Otelagh peers down upon me as I walk upon the trail that he leads me.

I sit and watch the last colors of Otelagh's pass fall across the waters from the heavens, and as the last light of day begins to turn to night I have a vision where I see a great Ehkolie, whale, rise from beneath the waters of the setting sun and sing a song of love and promise to the women of his village.

He too welcomes all those that compel his rise from beneath the deep waters as he shall lead them safely and that they too can become strong and vigilant, and independent from complaint as they tour safely beside him across the waters that has breathed life into all our beginnings.

The air is warm and the soft breaths of the east winds fall quietly across the land, and as darkness has touched the sky again, and the bad spirits begin to attempt to poach what is right in our souls, the Hyas Owl calls soundly unto the secretive hides where the evil spirit of the pishpish are known to dwell.

I know all life that shares this meadow tonight will be allowed to share of their spirit again upon Otelagh's return by the watchful eyes of our meadow's welcomed guard.

After this long day the scent of the Cedar bark is welcoming to my senses as it lays heavy upon the ground that I rest. As the fire grows with frenzy, within its many flames rises too the faces of all the animals and insects that I had seen on my trek this day. Each of them I see dancing together at the fringes of the fire's hearth, dancing as if they too are as one before the eyes of the Great Owl who watches all.

My eyes have grown weary and as I begin to drift to sleep, rising up from the center of the fire's reddened flame the muskrat brgins to dance upon his hind feet as he reaches out for my hand to take me to where he has chosen my lesson to be held. Yet, I know that the flame of the fire is where the muskrat's spirit chooses this night to dwell, and I know to dare not reach for his beckoning hand as my eyes are now closed. Yet, I am now lying moved to the muskrats needs, and I lay there unmoving yet moved by the Muskrat's spirit, I begin to see, and with extended fingers I begin to feel as if they were all for the first time given the day of my birth.

My senses became alive, and my mind was promised by the muskrat's dance to tell of my journey that I was to travel. I began to search my soul without knowing that it was the understanding of life and how each of our species would need one another to survive that muskrat was about to lead me. Upon each turn from the fire's flame that muskrat chose for his dance, a new chapter of my life evolved before me, yet, I did not understand how I would grow beyond the time a single night would offer me.

Chapter after chapter filled my mind as I slept. Each had its own story, each with their own beginning, and each with their own ending.

I was still to question unknowingly to all that I had been directed. From the Osprey to the Kokostick, from the elders to the muskrat. I was still lost to my vision. Lost to the reason for my trek to the opening of this marsh that lies low to the Birch and Cottonwood. Below the outstretched arms of the mighty Oaks, and where the screams of the Pishpish are gathered tightly to the growls of the Klale Lolo as they spell warning to those who trespass upon the lands wherein lie their darkened dens.

As I slept I could hear the muskrat speak softly in my ear as he danced within his flame. He spoke of the marsh where life meets death with opened arms, here life draws from the waters, here death lies silent and breathes life once again unto itself. With each season that Otelagh passes overhead, muskrat explained how we learn that death is only the announcement of new life to soon appear.

"Life is alike death!

Without life there could not be death, and without death there would never be need for new life to arrive before our doors."

"This is the circle of life."

"Life is ever changing!"

"Life wears many masks.

"It is we who must first discover its many faces and learn how to better understand where our commitments must lead us so that life shall never be pretended upon the light of day, but be seen in both, light and darkness."

"We must accept both to understand both!"

"These are our ways," said the muskrat.

Throughout the night I would awaken to place more wood on the fire, and as I rose up I felt as though I had new life breathed into my soul, and that each journey I would then travel from that day forward would be supported with greater energy. With a new outlook on life itself I would be chosen as life would lead our peoples to offer thanks to each of the Illahee's animals as they lead us through life safely if we step down from our own telecasit and stand beside their gathering as we witness to their own gifts that will in turn, teach us to the likeness of our own.

We are not the teachers upon Otelagh's Illahee, but we are to learn from the many animal's spiritual ways as they arrive before our paths as they were given life before our own first breaths were to be drawn.

Our intelligence must be opened toward a newed beginnings.

It shall be these same lessons that shall offer us fortitude before all our brothers as we pass one another upon the trails of life as we each are given to the journeys we will undertake in our individual quests of discovery.

This is the lesson that muskrat chose for me to follow from this night forward . . .

The day has begun with a new vision that I have yet to share. Golden light spreads across all the leaves of all the trees that line the entrance of the marsh as Otelagh sheds warmth across their bows.

Birds sing their love songs as they stand upon the highest branch of the tree of their choice.

As I sit up I can discern murmurs from all the animals and plants spreading softly across the meadow into the lands beyond the forest's entrance to my arrival before their opened door.

Sweet scent rises from the forest's floor and washes over me as it allows my senses to entertwine with the messages that are selectively sent before my feet.

I know this is not only a beginning of a new day, but it is the beginning of a new life, as my journey is soon to be fulfilled with a new recognition of where the Hyas Tahmahnawis directs my conceptions as I follow in his custom.

My feet march to his mighty drum through the mire as he leads me.

Taken by the beauty of the lands whereby I am surrounded, my eyes now see all that I had not seen, my fingers feel each blade of grass, each tree, each plant and flower without touching, I hear each sound as if I had been deaf in all the days that Otelagh had passed above me.

This day I find reason that it shall not be like any other I have shared before.

Muskrat is within me, and all that I thought yesterday is not what I shall know today. I sense that all I know today shall be multiplied, and upon the rise of Otelagh tomorrow, and my soul shall be filled with a better understanding to what is truly our gift in passage toward the exigency of seeing life upon its rightful stage for all our tomorrows.

Now that my eyes have opened and my heart can now feel the spirits that have always lain before my feet unnoticed, my walk now takes me along slow waters. Waters where the frogs and turtles are gathered amongst their own tribe as they lie silent upon the broken limbs and tout the warmth of Otelagh's leisurely travels above.

Beset by a passing breeze I view a limb that is cradled to the belly of the mighty Painted Turtle.

The turtle is told to offer faith in all that erases our confusion from the truths that our fathers and forefathers have spoken throughout our visage upon these lands. Once we gather Turtle Spirits within us, our complaints shall be taken from our souls and we shall once again be healed and see the wisdom of our father's ways.

Turtle is strong and viable! Turtle is where we take all that is good from within the Bad Spirit's grasp, and we trust in the Bad Spirit only to clench tightly to the emptiness of his wayward soul's most distressing call.

As Turtle slides silently into the waters of life, I too am taken from where my soul had once lost its vision, and new hope appears for all the tomorrows I had once questioned.

Where Turtle slid beneath the waters came forth the Carp. A mighty messenger who shows all that if we walk with opened eyes and hearts, that we will see beyond what lies before us, and all that Carp shows us shall bring honor amongst our gathering.

It has been told from the beginning that Carp ties life with love. Through our acceptance of Carp's arrival before us, our lives shall become fertile, and our efforts before our brothers that sit and share our fires shall then be seen with honor and respect. It is both, honor and respect that we must command if we are to be seen as worthy before the Hyas Tahmahnawis as we walk amongst his kingdoms and take the souls of the mowitch and moolack and pish so that we can place them upon our tables.

Through the arrival of Carp may we all one day rise before the Mighty Tumtum's gates and be seen upon the rise of the moon and be set free far into the darkness of night.

With Carp beside us, we will take all that life offers with our acceptance to all that it brings to our tables, and with life held solidly within our hearts shall soon be brought the escence of love within our souls. In that same love shall honor be brought as our young shall rise again in our essence, and our peoples shall live on upon these lands where we are now joined.

And Otelagh shall not dismiss his presence over our gathering upon these Lands of Wah . . .

I have walked upon many trails through the marsh as the Great Muskrat had chosen for me to follow, and as I leaned to rest upon the trunk of a Mighty Oak along the bank of the lake where I was taken, settled just above my shoulder, the Mighty Heron.

The Mighty Heron is the messenger of authority and advice, and as we exchanged our gaze, he began to share his wisdom to what I must do to strengthen my place amongst my peoples and before the chair of our Hyas Spirits.

Great Heron told of his own village, high up into the top most reaches of the trees, and this is where his tribe's village is found. Heron shared that here they could see far into the lands and watch over them with cautioned eyes towards the rise of danger upon the horizon's storm.

Great Heron knew of the drum's unending cadence across these lands as the winds carried our people's announcement of their misguided soul's directives leading to many wars that were then spread throughout the kingdoms wherein we were sadly drawn.

Great Heron spoke of justice; he spoke of honor; he spoke of faith. He spoke of all I had been taught upon my journey.

Great Heron spoke freely as he was the caretaker to this marsh, and all that he shared was then spelled to the marsh where his tribe was now held.

Great Heron feared as did the messenger that shared our camp's fire that journeyed from the east and spoke amongst us of new peoples who did not understand our ways, and how they would take from our lands and leave nothing in return.

He told of the water's rise as they would covet the marsh beneath their wake, and all that his tribe knew, would be no more.

Great Heron too shared his grief as did Great Cedar, in his not knowing of the tomorrows that we would soon face. It is those same tomorrows that he asks for me to share before the Walls of Wahclella and before our Forefathers, and to ask for their guidance to change the new people's thinking so that all that is now shall survive in all the tomorrows to follow.

I told Great Heron that I would share his story as I had promised Great Cedar, and through his council all the tribes that our drums could reach shall be apprised of the stories that I had been told. I told Great Heron that I would sit amongst our brothers and share of all the stories I had been told that life was once free from prejudice and that all spirits once reigned free from the disease that mankind willingly spreads.

I told Great Heron that as long as I lived amongst the spirits of these lands my voice would be heard each day, and every day it would be spread further and louder than the day before to reach out to those that do not share our heart.

This would be forewarning to those that insist to further their greed and thirst for all the gifts that belong to all the peoples of this Illahee.

Great Heron honored me with his trust, and as he flew off into the forest's hides where his tribe awaited word of our conference, I could see tears falling from his eyes as they streamed steadily upon the waters of the lake. I could not tell if they were of joy or fear, but even as I promised for my voice to be heard each day hereafter, I knew that the tribe that was soon to arrive before our doors were unjust, dishonorable, and had faith only in that they would not listen to our hearts.

I too found myself saddened that our days were now numbered, and all that we knew would change. It is that change that we must reconsider upon their souls, but in the end, there is death before life reappears upon all our tables . . .

It was my father's vision that I am now upholding that had approved of my name by the Hyas Tahmahnawis. Nenamooks, Land Otter, the one who walks on land and holds the totem of all life within his hands, the one who walks in honor of all that was and all that is . . .

My Totem allows me the strength to move forward in all my endeavours as today life itself has approved of my stance before all living beings. Through the versed lessons that I have been gifted upon this journey by all that appear beside my opened door upon the brother of my friend, Great Cedar, the Muskrat, the Osprey, the Goose, the Coyote, the Painted Turtle, the Carp, and the Great Heron tell that from death arises new life, and it is that same life that we must honor and respect, and not take its gift without knowing that it is as easily taken from us and not replaced if we do not open our minds and allow our hearts and souls to grasp each living being's reason to live safely amongst us.

Upon the Walls of Wahclella I was first versed to comprehend the importance of my life's journey. I was told to will our brother's understanding to the origins of life, and how our bondage toward the survival of all the plants and animals, large or small, will renew themselves upon life's mighty stage that arrives even after my spirit has passed on into the heavens if we have inherited the gift of respecting life in every form.

In all life there is no gift stronger than to love, and once we understand how to give our souls to life, we shall be able to enter onto the stage where love bars no man or woman from entering through its welcoming door.

It is then that we each can discover that to love is to better understand that all that is today shall always be tomorrow . . .

I understand now that the vision I have been blessed was chosen for my soul to become alike that to the shape of the pish, and now I have found my way home after journeying many moons before I have been able to discover the trail that leads me safely to my home waters.

The Hyas Eagle Feather now lies safely within me, and I with it, and all life shall forever walk in peace beside us once I share to all my brothers this vision that I have been honored.

Chapter 26
My Reward

The most significant teaching that the Hyas Tahmahnawis shared before me proclaimed that we must allow all life to discover their safe trace upon the Earth's lands.

Given one of my travels I had found myself entering the wetlands and where the Great River floods as the warmth of spring arrives upon us, and where our brothers had built their village of Cathlapotle. As I approached the shoreline of a lake its arms were lain outstretched from the marshy plain, and suddenly, arose from the stilled waters, a wounded kalakalama, goose.

Stunned, I stood and peered toward the distant shoreline as this gander quickly began to falter from her rise above the water's plane, and she suddenly toppled across the brush that stood staunchly upon the water's banks.

I was certain that a Talupus had earlier ensnared her within its jaws as many of her feathers had fallen from her wing as she flew to the far shores.

I quietly entered the marsh and began to listen for her movement, and as I neared her hide she attempted to escape through the thickness of the reeds, and as I reached out to capture her she began to beat me with her wings as she lay on her back hissing.

I quickly captured her and tethered her injured wing with vine that was growing along the edges of the marsh and then retraced my steps to my camp.

As I sat before the fire my soul was quickly warmed to the kalakalama's unspoken appeal.

I had faith that her injured wing might heal quickly if I were to bind it along her side in order that she could not attempt her escape again. As I cleansed her wounds and bound her injury, the kalakalama settled before our campfire and accepted my presence without fear showing in her eyes or through her actions beside me.

We settled alongside one another in our camp for three passes of Sun, and my eagerness to continue my journey began to allow me to become unsettled, yet the Counsel of Wahclella warned me that I must be attuned to the needs of all life and not just to those of my brothers.

Must I believe that this gander's encounter was chosen as a lesson by the Hyas Tumtum?

The kalakalama and I both sat before our camp for three more passes of Sun, and I began to grow curious as to why she chose to be silent rather than call upon all her brothers and sisters that flew above our camp.

On the seventh day as I inspected her wound I found her to be healed, though sadly, I also saw that many of the feathers had not yet appeared through the quills upon her wing.

This forced me to question the Hyas Tahmahnawis as I knelt upon the ground, and as I plead for the Hyas Tahmahnawis' explanation and to what I should do to further help in the healing of her wounds my wail before him was quickly answered.

"Nenamooks. You must take this gander to the shoreline and release her to the Chinook that arises above the waters of her capture."

With the Spirit's words now directing me I quickly gathered the Kalakalama under my arm and began our walk toward the shoreline, and as we neared the still waters she began to stir in my arms as she smelled the scents that were attached to the borders of the lake that she had become well known.

Then suddenly, the dew from the morning's cold breaths began to rise up from upon the water's of the lake and offered the souls of the lifeless spirits of the sticks soft beds of which to stand as smoke spirits layed heavy beneath their root, and as I witnessed to the beauty of this scene arising before me, a rich and colorful arch began to cross the heavens. With warm light cast down upon us, Otelagh had then shared his gift upon us pleasingly.

I knew this was a sign from the High Spirit that what was about to occur this day was to be alike no other day I had yet shared upon my visage to these lands.

As I stood upon the high bluff in awe and peered across the treasure of this lake, I took from my friends face the soft cloth that settled her in my arms, and I then with outstretched arms offered her to the breaths of the Chinook to gather beneath her wings.

As she took notice of her surroundings she once again settled in my hands as if afraid of the Talupus that once preyed upon her passive soul.

Rising upward the Chinook's breaths ran swiftly across the waters of the lake, and suddenly, without thought to the challenges she would soon face, I smiled as I offered hope and faith that she would one day bring new life to the Earth as I set her spirit free once more.

As I heaved my arms forward and thrust her toward the far shores of the lake she flew a short distance and glided safely upon the lake's mottled plane.

I stood happily before her as she once again gained freedom from her captivity.

Once she regained her senses as she peered across the waters of the lake I watched her swim to the far shore as she inspected her new home. As I was accepting that she had too accepted her place amongst the life that stirred of this lake, I slowly turned from the lake's shore and began to walk towards the forest's hides when her call loudly resonated upon the water's rush to the shore of the bluff.

As I turned to her, she called out proudly as she quickly swam below my point where I again stood facing her.

She appeared to honor my decision as she gathered the Chinook's breaths beneath her remaining feathers and stood upon the lake's surface, voiceing her excitement and pleasure toward her return and of her freedom to swim in the waters where she had once before chosen to be her home.

As tears held taut to the corners of my eyes I stood in admiration for my new friend's voiced acceptance of her return, and for her acceptance to me and of the efforts I offered to help her wounded wing to heal.

My soul was then touched beyond all the lessons that I had expected the Hyas Tahmahnawis had envisioned me to learn, and this moment was infinitely beyond approach to the words that I could ever explain before the peoples that I would meet upon my journeys from that day forward.

My heart lifted far from within my chest, and I exhaled deeply as the spirit that she and I then shared overwhelmed me.

We were then promised to one another, and as we each had clasped to the spirit that then moved within us, we silently bid one another good bye.

But in all this, my heart warmed to this kalakalama as she too knew of me and I then knew of her, and our souls were gathered, and we were then as one upon the Hyas Tumtum's Illahee and beneath Otelagh's pass above.

I chose to give life opportunity to flourish amongst us, and by her sounding upon the stilled air, the Great Chinook carried her message that I had then served upon the Hyas Saghalie Tyhee's most reverent lesson.

To honor life and accept its place beside us is to discover the power that love shall then hold within us forever as we journey along the trails of our brothers and sisters that the Hyas Tumtum had wished for us to find favor.

Many suns and moons have passed since that day, and the lesson that I had learned was not at first present within me to understand, but with the passing of my youthful ways and my entrance into manhood I had become aware to what a treasure she has become within my soul.

She and I shall always carry the memory of one another, and from within our souls, we each shall reach out and touch those that gift us with their presence, and they too shall carry the lesson that we share to those that they pass, and all life on this Illahee shall then one day become as one.

Life shall upon that single, most welcomed day, be then forever united, and our fears wrought by the Mesachie Tahmahnawis' beg for all our defeat shall disappear from our memories, and we shall prosper and our souls shall join, and each of our spirits shall be alike one to the Earth.

Just as my friend and I have become to one another for all eternity . . .

Robin Koster

305

Chapter 27
The Great Larch

Throughout the days that the Spirits have led me through the toils that our peoples have endured, I have begun to understand why there are both good and bad spirits, and through their teachings I have begun to learn of how to take from both so that we can better understand where the paths of each of their spirits may lead us. As we learn to adjust our thinking and become honorable below Otelagh we shall then silence forever the wail of the Mesachie Tahmahnawis for our souls.

As Otelagh rises upon his high trail I have begun my journey to the peak that overlooks all the Lands of Wah and of The Valley Of The Eagle, this tall telecasit we have named the Great Larch.

The Hyas Larch is told to have been a land where fire and smoke once filled the air above our lands and the spirits roared their dislike to their captivity below within the Mesachie Tahmahnawis', Bad Spirit's fiery tomb. A place where life could not find its breath as great smoke fell upon the lands. A place where fire spewed from the bad spirit's gaping mouth and led all life far from the Kloshe Tahmahnawis', Good Spirit's hold, and left only in their footprints ashes to be blown across our lands that were then buried beneath their soils where our peoples are now held.

This was a land where not even the Hyas Pishpish, Great Cougar or the Klale Lolo, Black Bear dared to enter.

This was a land held captive by the rise of Wy-East's bad spirit as the Earth trembled beneath his wakening.

A land where death's darkened face once ruled before all that dared entry upon its unshodden tracts.

One day the Great Larch fell silent as Otelagh passed overhead as he scolded the bad spirit of Wy-East for taking from his kingdom all life that had once reigned free from harm and far from the clinched fist that stood strong and merciless upon its peak that shared revulsion to all that Wy-East had pleasingly sired.

As Great Larch fell silent and the smoke had been cleansed from the heavens the Great Missoula fell from the north upon the kingdoms of the south and washed from their faces all the sticks and animal spirits, yet the spirit of Great Larch, the lost spirit of Wy-East, stood tall and high above the lands that were now drown beneath Missoula's distempered waste.

Below the high peak of Great Larch now began to rise from beneath their earthen binds the first saplings and kloshe tupso that would soon shed cover and color before the animal spirits that would once again gather to the meadow along the shores of the lake where it once gathered beneath his crown.

Great Larch had many brothers and sisters that stood distant to Wy-East's silken robe, and they too soon fell silent and crumbled to the soils of the Earth that lay at their feet. From the soils of each offered life's beginnings, and all the spirits that once surrounded Great Larch's brothers and sisters distasteful presence returned, and again life was renewed, and the Earth's rhythm was once again felt and heard through its soothing and swaying song.

It is this high place that I seek that oversees all the lands of our kingdoms, just as it has stood free from the many days of floods by Missoula's wasteful poach.

Great Larch had once fled from before the chair of the Kloshe Tahmahnawis of Wy-East and had quickly hid beneath the soils until he chose to rise up with the wrath of a medicine man that then chose to spread death from his depraved mind.

I see Great Larch's battle within himself to be alike that of our own in that the good spirit shall one day overcome the battle between the bad spirit and all that once was then shall be again as it was upon the first day of the land's birth.

From the gift of life follows death, and from death's saddened day rises life to again stand tall and mighty before all that appear and pass before it. This is the way that Great Muskrat chose for my story to be told.

Mankind is first seen pure upon our births, and as many of us encounter hardships and learn of greed and power, we soon falter before the storm that quickly inherits our souls, and many of us are not to return before the chairs of the good spirits.

This is why I climb to the high place where now rests the Great Larch. First I am to stand before all the Cascade Spirits and hear of their calling of my name as I stand high up on the Great Larch's crown, and then to look across our kingdom and see what has become of our lands once the bad spirit's spell had fallen from spreading fire and smoke upon the lands and burning the soils from where new roots have just begun to rise.

It is the way of our Illahee, Earth to begin anew, as it is our people's own. We first know of right and choose to what is wrong, and then it is that fight where often we see our brothers taken from our sides and are soon discovered lying upon the field's of sharpened rocks above the bad spirit's lowly tombs. The surviving brothers that had weathered their spiritless torrents now beg before the Hyas

Tahmahnawis for their acceptance to return before his chair and find shelter from the storm where the Mesachie Tahmahnawis has enjoyingly wreaked havoc within their souls.

These are our brothers and sisters that we can save from lying upon the bad spirit's table!

These are the brothers and sisters that we must catch first before they fall prey to the bad spirit's most enticing and taunting drum.

As I walk beyond the waters that have shone praise to the Multnomah's Great Chief's daughter as they have fallen from the high cliff from that sad day where she saved all the people's that had journeyed far to share in her joyous marriage,

I am now marked through the forest's sticks, and am swallowed within their majestic rise beside me upon the trail that leads to Great Larch.

Higher and higher I climb, each step I thrust forward brings me closer to my rise upon the high peak of Great Larch. It is here where I am to find the spirits of Wy-East, Mt. Hood, Lawala Clough, Mt. St. Helens, Pahto, Mt. Adams, Seekseekqua, Mt. Jefferson, Tahoma, Mt. Ranier, all joined together in wait for my arrival to our council.

Upon reaching the crest of Great Larch I peered across the kingdoms where lived my peoples and many of those from villages near our own that had shared our camp's fires. To these kingdoms rose up their High Spirits above all the valleys and canyons that were once formed by Otelagh's wishes as he toured the heavens and chose to give spirit to the lands as they rose up to the heavens to meet him each day.

Each were covered in their silken robes as they sat patiently upon their frozen bench, and from the feet of their bench flow the waters of their streams and rivers that are collected in their journey from the land's of their birth by the Great River far below.

These are the wates where the Hyas Pish are first bore, and to these waters are heralded to be where life has first begun, as the Hyas Spirits that firmly stand upon Wahclella's wall has spoken.

In the beginning there was only darkness, so The Hyas Tumtum gave the spirit of light to Otelagh so that he could shine down upon all the lands. As Otelagh gave rise the second day Hyas Tumtum saw nothing but desert and hot steam rising from the tepid lands below. His tears fell hurriedly upon the lands as he was saddened that there was no life that would honor him, and as each day passed the soils began to turn from the dry and desolate lands where the bad spirit dwells to the lands that have now changed into the bountiful meadows and valleys where stand proudly our forest's sticks, and where beneath lie greening beds of moss and fern.

Each passing day that Otelagh soared above the lands the Hyas Tumtum honored his rise above the lands and breathed life into the elk and deer, to the coyote and the fox, to the mosquito and to the mighty dragonfly.

Before the sixth day had passed Hyas Tumtum had placed all the spirits that we know today upon our Illahee for us to first honor and then for our peoples to take only those spirits that will offer us our survival below Hyas Tumtum's son, Otelagh's watchful pass overhead.

As all the days that we have known is now approaching the seventh day, the day when the old medicine men tell of dark clouds approaching across the horizons.

The day that will turn to night and Otelagh will not pass overhead once more. The day when summer will turn to winter and we will all be held prisoner within our lodges, and our souls will freeze and our hearts shall stop, and all that we had become will forever be unseen and unknown as there will be no one to follow in our footprints that will then not lend themselves by our lead.

This is the day when we, and all our brothers, must prove to all the Kloshe Tahmahnawis' of our Illahee that our souls are not chosen to the Mesachie

Tahmahnawis that has dared us to step into his realm.

We must ask ourselves to where our own footprints have taken us?

Have we journeyed through our lives learning of what is right? Or, have we journeyed throughout our lives accepting to what is wrong?

These are the choices that we have inherited.

As you sit before the fire that is lit this night, ask:

"Where have I gone?

"What have I seen?

"What have I learned that will allow my soul to see beyond into the rise of Otelagh upon the eighth day?

"Will it be you that has learned to what is right and has survived, or is it you that has accepted wrong and will not be seen nor heard again?"

Chapter 28

My Return Before the Chairs
of Our Guardians

Many years have passed since the first day I stood bewildered before the Counsel of Wahclella, and as this day's sun rises from behind the faces of our highest peaks, I hear far off into the distance, riding on the winds across the great river, my name called as my esteemed leader's voices have settled before my feet. As I stand and listen to our forefather's message as they each take upon their turn, they have requested for me to stand before their Council once more before the Walls of Wahclella.

I have stood before our chiefs many times from that first day throughout my term as the leader to my village, and I too find myself alike the Hyas Pish that returns home and is gifted to breath new life into their tribe before they are to pass on to their wintered villages, and once I retrace my steps to my village and share of my witness to our father's vision before all my brothers and sisters, we each are alike the offspring of that same Hyas Pish Tahmahnawis as we venture forth upon the trails of this Earth and find our travels upright and true before each and every of our great father's wishes as we offer new life through their vision.

I have discovered that man is not much different than all the animals that surround us, as each of our souls are connected and we all bring to one another gifts that only we each can share.

The chill of winter's breaths have collected solidly within me these past years, and as my name is now called, I am ready to accept what it is that our Forefathers may ask of me, and I shall, with honor and dignity, accept wherever they may ask for my new journey to be pointed.

I find within my soul that I am readied to pass on the highest honor I have been bestowed by the Hyas Tahmahnawis to whom holds within their soul the strength to withstand all obstacles that will hide amongst the shadows of their journeys upon our Illahee, and if this day is to be my last, it shall only shine brightly below Otelagh's passing light, whether it be to this day or to the approaching darkness of this night.

My heart is happy that my son is readied for his trial before the Hyas Spirits, and if I were to ask of my choice for the name of our new leader that would safely lead our peoples into the days beyond our own, I would wish that it be my son, Towagh Leloo, Bright Wolf.

I know he would safely lead our peoples through all the trials that they will be misfortuned to encounter as many peoples from far distant lands shall arrive before our doors and settle upon us, not as our neighbor, but as our conquerors.

I fear they shall will their own beliefs upon our peoples and take from upon our lands what is all ours to share as it was intended upon Otelagh's first pass over his lands as he offered his breath to be blown into all the plants and animals as they each were gifted upon the Earth from the beginning.

I have no fear that my son's heart would change from the ways of our fathers and lead our peoples into battle, as he too, as myself, have always chosen the way of understanding first the plight of others, and as we grasp that understanding and spill it slowly within the shell of patience, that it too shall one day lead to forgiveness, and then all our brothers shall join hands as peace between all our tribes shall once again find our prosper beneath Otelagh's passing above.

My eyes have become weary and my heart heavy as I have seen many battles fought without a victor to either camp. It has never been seen that when there are two that wish to join in battle that either walks away unscathed once their battle has begun. I have often thought that it is not the fallen soul that is darkened and held sorrowful, but it is the victor's soul that is forever sorrowed in the darkness' unknowing of his own memory by the taking of his brother.

It is as if Bright Wolf knows of my calling from across the waters of our Great River as he arrives from our village beside me carrying two paddles. Bright Wolf must believe that he too shall join alongside me as I bow beneath the Council of Wahclella and be chosen to their wish. But as he stands beside me with concern spilling from within his eyes I tell him that this is a journey that only I can take as the Council has summoned my name alone to stand before them and hear of their address.

To know that my name has been announced to enter into the valley beneath the falls of Wahclella, and for me to stand before the chairs of our forefathers and take from their purse to what they shall awardingly offer me, and to bring prosper and fortitude to our peoples, grants me strength to rise up and grasp upon the very spirit of life itself as my first step is quickly followed by my second and then my third as I walk to the shore where my canoe awaits.

As I gather the wind behind me and accept the river's driven wave that propels me to the shores where Wahclella's stream drops into its fast waters, I accept the honor the Council has wished for me without question.

I find that the honor they have bestowed upon me is alike the sun as it rises from behind the screen of darken clouds of winter's storm, and that sun has shed its warmth deep unto my soul. I am alike a new man, young and vigorous to my quest before them, but through the days of my past lessons, I am now reserved and poised as I begin a new passage upon the soils of these imposing Lands of Wah.

As my feet once again touch the soils upon the river's bank beside Wahclella's stream after many suns have passed safely overhead from my last journey before them, I find myself peering closely to all that lives along the trail's beginning as I recall the spectacle that honorably awaits my arrival before the feet to the Walls of Candor.

As I stand before the opened gates to Wahclella as I near the site where Munra falls, my wail is cast before the Council's gathering far ahead from where my voice is lent to the heavens, and upon the completion of my pleading words a voice arises from above the sticks of our forest and is heard to offer;

"Klahowha, Welcome To Our Lodge!"

As I walk along the creek that leads to the Walls of Candor and before the chairs of our forefathers I pass Munra's plunging fall and begin my climb upon the trail that leads to our gathering potlatch.

As I climb higher into the canyon where Wahclella and our forefathers await my presence, I begin to recall my first trek within this beautiful valley so long ago.

It was a journey through all the suns and moons that our peoples had been chosen to these lands, and to those brothers that sacrificed their own selfish pursuits in life and accepted the quest that our great leaders had chosen for their lead, our forefathers gave honor to each of their names as they spoke highly of their tributes before them.

We have honored the Coucil of Wahclella just as has Otelagh honored us within his kingdom. For it was from the beginning that Otelagh chose for our peoples to rise up and be one with the Hyas Illahee, and not be drawn to introduce harm or devestation to linger across our lands, as we had promised to spread the Council's wish to life's prosper and our commitment to one another's survival as Otelagh first passed overhead as we knelt along the fast waters of our great river.

All that I have become has been treasured to my soul through the very teachings that have been dispursed before me, and through those teachings as I have come to interpret them, their significance to others that we have passed and have shared of their story before our village's fires has been manifest within them.

Upon the innocence of a summer's day the songbirds announce their joy as I walk beside them. Both, them and I, bask in the warmth of a new day's sun, and as I strive higher to again cross the waters of Wahclella's stream, enlivened by life itself, we each open our hearts without prejudice and share happiness to all life that passes before us as the summer breeze's breaths spread the sweet scent of the flower's pollen upon us.

Each of us, enthralled within our own thoughts.

Innocent and Free!

Suddenly, in a blink of time's recording, all the happiness we had just shared, all the smiles that we had just extended have been extinguished beneath a darkened cloud now swollen from upon the soils of our harried Earth.

With deaf ears we listen, with blind eyes we see.

We ask given our ascension before Death's Cradle,

"Where are we, and what have we done?"

In a flash in time all that we know today would be quickly lost!

Our Innocence.

Our Freedom.

And in those same moments can be heard our silenced cry,

"Why?"

Many of our brothers have in turn become wise to the exigency that life itself presents as we walk amongst its treasured hold.

Once we have elected to open our hearts and see beyond the visions wrought by our blinded eyes to what lies fronting us today, all our tomorrows can rise up with the promise for another tomorrow to follow.

I find that it shall be those tomorrows that we are about to find others to their question.

This I fear as has our forefathers that have stood unopposed upon the cliffs before Wahclella's plunge.

I recall the visionary that shared our fires as he shared of many men soon to witness of our lands, and that they would not understand or accept the message that we were to share before them.

In their haste to capture the spirit of these lands they shall take away much that shall never return within our kingdom's treasured hold, and all that our kingdom had once been treasured shall not be seen again . . .

I fear once these brothers appear upon our horizon that they shall look upon these lands as untamed, and they shall then take from upon the Illahee many animal spirits that we have learned to live amongst as it is their souls that lead us in safety upon our travels.

I too have seen the Hyas Eagle and the Klale Lolo, the Hyas Pishpish, and the Coyote spelled from our lands, and in their loss, we too shall lose our direction for it has been their spirits that drive our understanding that life itself, be it to animal or to man, is to be accepted and necessary to further each of our own survival upon our Illahee.

We have learned much from the animal spirits that thrive amongst us, and we shall be lost upon their trails without their calling for all the days that pass once they have chosen to another's trail.

And they shall not be seen again . . .

It shall be to our loss as our own spirit shall then be lost to us, and we will not reign free from these new people's pestilence and disease.

Then too, our villages shall be lain in waste as will be our vision that Wahclella had once honored our travels across the Hyas Illahee of Wah.

And then we shall never be seen again upon these lands, as we shall be chosen upon another's trail, far from the lands where we had once discovered our honor before the Hyas Otelagh's reign above . . .

Given to one of my visions there is a single word that rests unsettled in my thoughts that these new peoples shall preach to their brothers of the east. It shall be often shared in how they see our likeness through their unheeded vision of all our people's tribes, as our beliefs are not alike their own.

In this, I fear they will choose not to hear our cry.

As black as the unlit night of the moon's absence within our heavens is what I hear called in our likeness to themselves in my vision by these peoples as they scream, "Renegades!"

"Why do they fear us?"

"Why do they fear what they do not understand?"

But as I have sat alone many nights and have taken heed of their conceptions to what this land may offer them, I find myself to ask,

"Is it truly our peoples that are the renegades that you speak?

Is it our peoples that reign free without thought to all those tomorrows where we each can share and teach one another of all the spirits of these lands where we have offered our bond as we stand free of their capture?

"Is it not you and those that follow in your steps and tread hardened across these lands that reneges on surrendering your greed for all that our land's hold within them?

"As your recklessness and greed take from our lands its treasure that Otelagh had first honored us once we promised to honor it and leave it untouched and unharmed from our forefather's beginnings, what will become of us, and will we each survive your thoughtless err?"

I sense these peoples are led by a different drum and their forefather's ideals are secured within their souls, as are our own. But as they are new to the ways of the Earth, they will be blind and corrupted as their forefathers have elected to leach from our Earth and give back nothing in return.

Through all the years of my lead before the peoples of my village I have never felt the need or cause for war, but this is now in question as we must then protect the ways of our Hyas Spirits.

"These peoples shall be presented with our trust, yet I fear our brothers across their kingdoms shall join arms and see these people's complaint without prejudice as these intruders cast lies before us all, and in our brother's haste, they shall take arms in defense to life itself as we know it today.

We shall quickly choose to join armies alongside the Mesahchie Tahmahnawis' many arms.

This I fear shall take our peoples nearer to our own eviction from the trails that we once knew and treasured.

And we shall not be seen upon them again . . .

This I fear shall take away all that has prospered proudly upon these lands!

These lands may not be seen again . . .

It has been the past battles between our brothers that has brought shame to our tables and sadness to our hearts, and the battles that we will soon fight against the new peoples that are soon to arrive before our doors shall bring darkness' chill across all our lands and promises to invest fear within our souls.

In this alone, I have learned to dread fear itself, as it shall become the end of all that we know upon Earth.

Our forests shall wilt from the madness that Otelagh will be committed to bare down upon their soils!

The cole breaths of winter shall freeze hardened to every corner of the Earth and outlast Spring's wanting return!

Our Illahee shall also tremble callously within its own complaint!

All that we have known shall be forever lost beneath its ruinous and earthen storm!

Great floods shall wash over our lands and take all that is anchored upon its path beneath its fastened wake!

The Illahee shall be no more as the Great Desert shall arise from the depths that lie beneath our seas!

All that we have known shall be forgotten as there shall be no one to share to what once was!

This is what I have come to dread in my vision!

Otelagh will one day pass overhead and bare down upon us his fee for our indiscretions towards the gifts that he had bestowed honorably upon us all!

This is where my vision has left me, troubled to what lies beyond where no one is left to share what once was!

"Beyond darkness' darkened shadow lies only darkness!"

Where hope and prosperity had once spread light upon all our visions now lies the darkness of night where only the Bad Spirits dare to exhibit their complaint to those that stride free from our Good Spirit's lead!

It is this same darkness that my eyes are now spelled as my strength has escaped my legs as I kneel before the Council of Wahclella and cry out before them to the vision that I have witnessed.

My thoughts are now pointed to all those that I have spoken. To my son, Bright Wolf, so that he can now become honored before all the peoples of our tribe, and that he will follow in our forefather's steps across this majestic land.

To my closest friend and the woman that I have loved deeply, Pupseela, and that she can see her son become the man that we know he would become, and to make her proud as she has earned the praise that she will be honored from all those that will soon surround her!

To Great Cedar, as he must hear my wail as his mother once wailed before the Spirits for her honor to reach far into the heavens of Otelagh's trail, and that he shall stand untouched to the day that he too shall join alongside his mother beneath the soils of their birth.

The burden that all my brothers shall one day encounter has been speared within my soul, and as my last breaths escape me, I must wail before your Council once more and thank you for the honor that you had bestowed upon my shoulders as you chose me to lead our peoples safely in all our father's vision.

"My fathers, to have seen all those tomorrows that you had spoken has brought me before you and has now chosen me to my knees as I praise your ways before your station upon these sacred Walls where Wahclella has cleansed our thoughts and has given us hope.

"As my time nears to walk amongst the trails of our heavens, and as the Hyas Coyote announces to all our peoples that my time to depart beside them has arrived across all the kingdoms that we have

shared, I am ready for your lead to where my soul shall be awardingly attached.

"May peace always surround our peoples, and may they follow in our strides across all the lands they encounter so that they too can see of all those tomorrows that we shall share upon Otelagh's next rise above . . ."

"My peoples, hear my cry,"

"Nika mitlite halo elite!"

"I Am Free!"

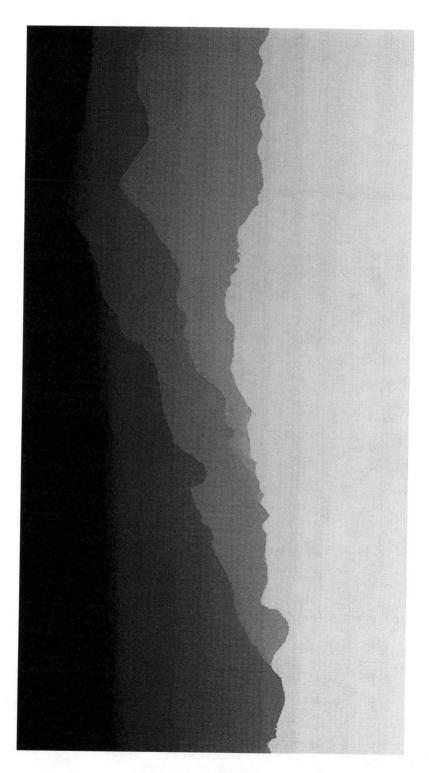

Chapter 29

To Have Seen the Sun of Tomorrow's Day

"Kopa Mitlite Nanitch okoke Otelagh of Tomolla Halo Polaklie"

"My Brothers!

"As the warmth of the day's sun has fallen from the heavens and the cold of night approaches, my life has now passed through the avenues of all the suns and moons that have stained the heavens above you, and my mortal spirit shall be soon routed unto the clutches of the Hyas Saghalie Tyee as I shall then be aligned with all my brothers that have chaired before our people's council.

"My spirit shall be taken upon the Hyas

Chinook's breaths as has many a fallen leaf that had sailed across the great river and had began to take seed upon the distant shore.

"My tutoring before the Hyas Spirits and my address before my brothers that I had crossed paths has begun a change in their awakening towards all charges from those that are not blessed by the gift of our dominion.

"The Hyas Saghalie Tyee had appointed my path upon earth to save the entirety of all the forms of life that had been bore upon the Great Illahee from the beginning that our brothers have been blessed to share. Upon my reception before the spirits of these grounds my teachings have led my peoples, you my brothers, to find the answer of your worth before the Great Spirits.

"My belief in the Hyas Spirit's philosophies has permitted my obedience to be lain before their demands, and as I have accepted their wisdom and have spread their words upon the paths that I have chose before all that have stood before me, my beliefs have allowed me to soar above our Illahee's domains and have permitted my individuality to rise and become independent from mankind's afflictions. Just as are the souls of the Hyas Chak-Chaks' as they soar beneath the heaven's gateways and peer down upon the soils that are spread magnificently beneath them.

"As each seed brings life upon our lands from all the earth's species, you, the caretakers of our Illahee must not portend that one species is of diminutive importance to the continuation of all life that this Earth supports upon the Saghalie Tyee's kingdom.

"Our brothers must survive with all other species upon Earth's face, and by your acceptance of their standing, life shall thrive throughout all the suns and moons that pass above your blessing upon the shores of the Hyas Columbia.

"Mankind must be determined to overcome all indifferences that are sorely placed before them by those tainted toward the wishes of our Hyas Saghalie Tyee!

"We must be ready to attach our triumph to the vestiges that stand magnificently before us!

"Toward these same tracings we must be concerted given our symphony to the treasures that this Earth is blessedly adorned.

"We, as humanity, must not be found wandered upon our lands as are the fallen meteors of our heavens!

"We must be taken by our invitation upon this Great Earth as we discover the sacred grounds we encounter!

"We must not be led astray from the gravity of their burnished and most honorable paths!

"I ask you my brothers upon my passing to the land of our High Spirits, choose your souls to be as dynamic as ours, and you shall be lodged in spirit alongside our own.

"As you are joined in your labors to follow in our vision, we shall all be remembered through the legends that are decided by our traces permitted upon our Illahee.

"Do not let pass our vision.

"As you emerge before the peoples that choose their stance upon our majestic lands, may their lessons be compellingly influenced by the truths that you profoundly speak!

"We Shall Honor the Earth and the Heavens!

"We Shall Honor Mankind!

"We Shall Honor the Spirits Bore to the Earth's Trails!

"If your spirit stands proud and wise before the Hyas Saghalie Tyhee's inspirations upon the paths you follow throughout the travels of your life, you may one day be promised to be observed crossing the heavens as do the Hyas ChakChak!

"Your spirit on that unparalleled day shall then be seen proudly stationed upon the Saghalie Tyhee's chosen star as it glistens with your ascension before the gates of The Highest Spirit's Castle, and as you rise above your brothers, you too shall be accepted by the Hyas Saghalie Tyhee, To Have Seen the Sun of Tomorrow's Day . . ."

"Kloshe Tumtum mika Chako."
"Welcome."

Chapter 30
Epilogue

Descending gracefully from the heights dominating far above the valley's floor, plummeting with their incredible forces to the avenues of the sea, we find the source of our amazement. A diversity of the world's most beautiful and dramatic waterfalls as they cascade some 1500 feet above the lush vegetation and meld with the Columbia River.

Here you will find these streams flowing through these majestic lands as they cleanse the air and give birth to the many varieties of fauna that lie upon the serene grounds specific to their creation.

Above all else, they are given to our souls as we stand in awe of their formidable presence as we explore unto their gravity as it pertains parenting upon our impressions.

This incredible, seemingly untamed land we find irreplaceable is known as the Columbia River Gorge National Scenic Area, that was established on November 1, 1981.

Wahclellaspirit

337

Photography
by
Steve Warnstaff

Vancouver, Washington

(360) 356-8459

warnstaff.photography@gmail.com

Pacific Northwest
Tours and
Workshops

Landscape and Art Prints

Steve Warnstaff